The Human Side of Budgeting

Budget Games & How to End Them

SCOTT DOUGLAS LAZENBY

Erehwon Press

Sandy, Oregon

Production, marketing, typesetting and cover design by
Erehwon Press.
Cover illustration from iStockPhoto.com.
Printing, sales & distribution by CreateSpace (an Amazon
company).

ISBN: 1490316094
ISBN-13: 978-1490316093

CONTENTS

PREFACE

Most current books on government budgeting focus on the **policy** process for making budget decisions. They also focus almost exclusively on the federal budget. *The Human Side of Budgeting* instead approaches the budget from a local government **management** point of view, and makes the case that traditional budget systems work against almost everything we know about good management (i.e., that most of our employees are not, in fact, lazy and stupid).

The Human Side of Budgeting was written both for pre-career students of public management as well as more senior managers who wonder why their budgeting systems produce such pathological behavior in their staff and governing bodies.

1

INTRODUCTION

Over sandwiches in a local pub, a reporter for the Oregonian newspaper interviewed the city manager and finance director of the City of Sandy. In the midst of the worst recession since the Great Depression, this small city in the foothills of Oregon's Cascades mountain range seemed to be performing an economic miracle. The housing market had collapsed, and other cities were laying off planners and building inspectors. Sandy was not only keeping its small planning and development staff intact, but the department still had a healthy reserve that would allow it to weather several more years of a permit revenue drought. The planners stayed busy updating long range plans, cleaning up the development code, and working with businesses on downtown development. The building official was applying his skills in managing upgrades to city buildings.

Other city councils had just completed a tortuous budget

setting process (in Oregon, the cities' fiscal year begins on July 1), deciding among the least painful of a set of cuts to staff and programs. In Sandy, programs remained intact, and the city council had actually been able to add to a few programs, confident that the resources would be there, in the long term, to support them.

While the municipal bond market was in turmoil, Sandy was in the process of issuing a few million dollars in urban renewal bonds (as general obligation bonds, backed by the city's "full faith and credit"). Standard and Poor's had just given the bonds a double A rating, the same as for the much larger City of Portland and the State of Oregon itself, and almost unheard of for a city of under 10,000 population. The rating agency had been impressed both by the level of financial reserves, and the city's financial management policies.

Sandy's economy was hit as hard as others. In fact, the city had doubled in population in just two decades, and much of the local economy was tied to the housing and development industry. That industry was now in shambles. On a per-capita basis, the property tax base (and other revenues) were relatively modest. The only clear difference between Sandy and most other Oregon cities was the way it managed its budget.

The two staff members explained the process to the reporter. Instead of having departments go through the game-playing of a competitive budget request process, the city manager gave each department director a set amount of general tax resources (based on a projection of how much would be available to balance the budget). They were then free to build their own budgets, adding any departmental revenues (fees, grants, etc.) they could, along with 100% of any savings carried over from the previous year. They were given complete control over line items, and were encouraged to set aside reserves in departmental contingency accounts to handle emergency repairs or cyclical revenues.

Because the operating managers were responsible for both expenditures and their own revenues (including the most volatile sources such as building permits, planning fees, and grants), they were expected to respond directly when expenditures and revenues didn't behave exactly as projected (the best budget is, after all, nothing more than an educated guess on what the future will hold). This allowed the city to use a 24-month budget period, freeing the staff and city council from the number crunching burden of an annual budget. The city council set overall goals for programs and service levels, but the responsibility for managing the budget was not centralized, and was instead delegated to the operating units within the organization.

This made life easier for the city council and executive staff. More surprising, the operating managers liked it, in spite of almost two decades of a fairly severe diet of general tax revenues. Rather than spending their energy and creativity figuring out how to out-compete their fellow managers for a share of the budget pie, they instead looked for ways to save money and boost revenues within their own departments. They appreciated having both the responsibility for financial management as well as the authority (and tools) to truly manage their own budgets.

The reporter wasn't an accountant, but she was familiar with the public spectacle that characterized the budget processes of the state and most other governments. She grasped the way a decentralized budget management system provided built-in mechanisms to monitor and respond to changing economic conditions, and how operating managers had a strong incentive to be as efficient as possible.

"Why," she asked, "don't more cities do it this way?"

Why indeed? It is not simply an issue of financial controls and accounting: proper accounting controls can be put in place in both a centralized and decentralized budget management system. It isn't that local government managers are ignorant of these concepts: several of the principles were highlighted two decades ago in Osborne and Gaebler's Reinventing Government (under the label "expenditure control budgeting"). It isn't that city councils enjoy the traditional budget jousting and gamesmanship; most individuals on city councils find the process frustrating and tiresome.

The answer to this question goes to the heart of management theory, and to the history of government management in the United States.

2

THE ROOTS OF BUDGETING IN THE REFORM AND PROGRESSIVE MOVEMENTS

A hundred years ago, as America entered the 20th century, two forces came together to change local government. The reform movement sought to address widespread corruption within city governments, and to put an end to the spoils system in which the city's political machine would reward supporters with city jobs and contracts. At the same time, the progressive movement held that an effective and efficient city government would be critical in addressing an increasingly urban population. Principles of the new administrative science that was being developed in the private sector could also be applied to government organizations, putting government on a scientifically sound and rational base.

A key feature of government reform was a strong centralized command-and-control management system. The work of Frederick Taylor had shown that work could be done much more efficiently if a smart manager could study the work processes, and then direct the workers in the best way to accomplish tasks.

The council-manager plan, championed by Richard Childs and the National Civic League would replace party bosses and political hacks with a professional (and ethical) central administrator, patterned very closely after a business CEO. An elected city council would still set overall policies and laws for the city, but an organizational firewall between policy and administration would reduce the opportunities for corruption. In 1924, the City Managers Association adopted its first Code of Ethics. To this day, adherence to this strict code remains the *only* requirement for a city manager to be a member of the professional association (now called the International City/County Management Association, or ICMA).

The first city managers tended to come from a background in engineering or business management.[1] They moved quickly to establish central purchasing and contracting departments, where vendors would be selected based on open bidding processes. Central personnel offices ensured that hiring and promotions would be based on merit, rather than on personal or political connections. Nepotism policies further limited the actual and perceived influence of family ties in personnel matters.

---

[1] Leonard D. White, *The City Manager* (Chicago, Ill.: The University of Chicago Press, 1927), ix-x.

Like purchasing and personnel, financial management practices were improved through formal organizational structures and processes. Cities typically handled finances the way many families do: if there was money in the bank account (or cash drawer), they could spend it. By today's standards, there was relatively little planning done on how the money would be spent, and little effort made in tracking how it was spent.

In 1901, the National League of Cities proposed a "uniform system" of accounts that could be used to track revenues and expenses, and to assist in making comparisons across cities. The new double-entry accounting systems tracked revenues and expenses, assets and liabilities, and provided both monthly and annual financial reports. "Thus there is outlined a business-like way of keeping business accounts. For carrying on the financial affairs of a municipality does not differ materially from the process of conducting an ordinary business undertaking."[2]

The reforms included not only new processes, but also new (centralized) organizational structures. "...a municipal accounting system cannot be satisfactorily carried on for a long term of years upon modern uniform lines unless sustained by correctly drawn ordinances of the city which shall give authority to the proper officers, who shall thereafter be held responsible for the practical working of the system."[3] This officer was often a city auditor; today the role is typically held by a finance director, chief accountant, or controller (an especially appropriate title).

Adoption of a budget as both a planning tool and formal

---

[2]Commercial & Financial Chronicle, 1905, Volume 81 No. 2108, p. 1463
[3]Ibid.

limit on spending was a key feature of these "business-like" cities. The line-item budget, to this day, the workhorse of budgeting, matched the account code structure of the "uniform system" (at least as far as revenues and expenditures were concerned). The final budget adopted by the governing body established *appropriations* that served as an upper limit for spending by operating departments. These limits were set by line item (e.g., office supplies), or by groups of line items (e.g., supplies and services).

As with the new accounting systems, the new approach to budgeting brought with it a centralized organizational structure for developing and managing the budget. The chief executive officer (city manager in the National Civic League's model form of government) played a key role in proposing a budget to the city council that he (100 years ago, all city managers were men) felt best met the needs of the city. This budget would represent a rational approach to carrying out the business of the city in a rational and efficient manner. The city council could make changes, and if the budget was completely at odds with their policy direction, they could simply fire the city manager.

Once the budget was adopted by the city council, the chief executive was accountable for managing it. If the city council set appropriations at a higher level (by department or program), the city manager (or finance director) could still set limits at the line item level, requiring operating departments to seek formal approval to shift budget authority between line items. In some cases, the fiscal year was split into smaller periods (months or quarters), and budget *allotments* limited total spending within these periods.

These reforms spread to the national and state

governments, with a vengeance. The concept of merit-based hiring and promotions became enshrined (some would say entombed) in the federal civil service system. Many states now participate with cities in complying with standards set by the Government Finance Officers Association of the United States and Canada (GFOA) for production of a budget document and a comprehensive annual financial report, and by the Governmental Accounting Standards Board (GASB) for accounting. The national government has struggled more in this area.[4]

As a sign of their zeal for business-like budgeting practices, state legislators often impose budget rules on local governments that are more stringent than those followed by the state government itself. In the State of Oregon, for example, local governments are required (by state law) to hold budget discussions in open public meetings, and to publish budget details in local newspapers. In contrast, budget decisions are made by the state government in secret caucus meetings and there is little useful public information until well after the budget is adopted.

A Typical Budget Cycle

The basic steps of the budget process have changed little in the century since the beginning of the reform movement. *Within* the budget cycle, governments have experimented with many gimmicks and innovations-du-jour (PPBS, zero-based

---

[4]See *Statement of the Acting Comptroller General of the United States*, General Accounting Office, 2010 (accessed at http://www.gao.gov/financial/fy2010/10gao1.pdf on 12/23/11)

budgeting, etc.) to lend an air of rationality to the messy political process of budget decision-making by the governing body. These have not had an effect on the budget process itself.

Step 1 (optional)
The governing body and staff use some kind of process to solicit citizen input on the priorities for the government. In local governments, this may culminate in formal goals set by the governing body.

Step 2
The chief executive officer (or designated staff, such as a finance director or budget officer) prepares instructions for departments in preparing their budget requests, typically in the form of a *budget manual*. Due to the increasing complexity of the budget process, this is often done long before the actual beginning of the fiscal year (as much as two years before, in the case of biennial state budgets).

Step 3
Operating departments prepare budget *requests*. Regardless of how budget decisions will be packaged for the governing body, the building block of a departmental request is a line item budget. In estimating the amount that will be needed for each line item, the department staff review spending trends, and make adjustments based on expectations for the future (e.g., inflation, or changes in service demand). Because these estimates are made far in advance of actual spending, the exercise is similar to driving a car down a highway by looking out the rear window using a telescope. And because the

departmental request will be subject to an internal competition for available funds, it is in this step that budget game playing is initiated (see Twenty-One Budget Tricks in Chapter 4).

Step 4

It is almost inevitable that budget requests will exceed the total amount of revenue available. The only exception occurs when the budget instructions place limits on each department's request, but in this case, the department's budget transmittal memo will emphasize the dire consequences of actually adopting a budget with such an unreasonably small appropriation. The chief executive officer, assisted by central finance staff, will oversee some kind of process (often including internal budget hearings) to get the budget to balance. In some cases, the CEO will be open to "revenue enhancement" (tax or fee increases), but more typically, the budget balancing process is a zero-sum game in which some departments win and some lose.

Step 5

The CEO formally transmits a *proposed budget* to the governing body. It is (at least for states and local governments) a balanced budget, so if the governing body wants to spend more on a given program, it needs to cut somewhere else, or increase estimated revenues.

Step 6

The governing board goes through some kind of process to arrive at a final budget. In many cases, this includes another set of budget hearings, in which departments vie for more money.

Step 7

The governing body adopts a budget, and sets legal appropriations.

Step 8

The CEO or designated representative sets further rules and limitations, and circulates the final budget limits to operating managers.

Step 9

Operating managers attempt to stay within spending limits, sometimes employing additional budget tricks to do so (for example, by charging travel expenses to the printing line item when the travel budget is used up).

Step 10

Central finance staff monitor spending by operating departments. They also monitor all revenue, including revenues generated directly by operating departments (e.g., licenses, user fees, grants), since most governmental accounting systems lump all revenues in a single place (the "general fund black hole," as it is known by operating managers). If revenues fail to meet estimated levels (not unusual in states, where a common tactic for balancing the budget is simply to inflate the revenue estimates), the central staff imposes new spending rules on departments.

Step 11

Budgeting in the public sector was meant to make

government more business-like, but business budgets are *plans*, not legal limits. If the government's spending plan, set long before the fiscal year began, turned out to be wrong, the process to amend the plan is often a tortuous one. Where spending limits are set administratively (in the case of budget allotments or line item controls), a central budget czar often presides over amendments. If a change in the legal appropriation limit is needed (even if revenues come in higher than estimated, or spending in other areas is well under budget), the government must go through a process of (typically) public hearings and budget resolutions.

Step 12

The fiscal year ends, and the books are audited. The Comprehensive Annual Financial Plan (CAFR) notes the difference between budgeted and actual amounts by fund and program. Operating managers pay little attention, because by the time the CAFR is published, they are well into another fiscal year, and preparing the budget for the next one.

In this process, the key budget decisions are reserved to the CEO and central finance staff, and the governing body. The operating managers are players in the game, but share little of the responsibility for balancing the budget. Once the budget is adopted, the rules of the game set up an adversarial relationship between the operating managers and the central finance staff, in which the operating managers are assumed to be profligate spenders, and the finance department is there to rein them in.In some organizations, wily operating managers actually fare well under this kind of process.[5]

Benefits of Budgeting in the Reform Era

The main theme of this book is that the reform era's budgeting practices have outlived their usefulness. But we shouldn't lose sight of the fact that they have been instrumental in bringing professionalism, accountability, and some amount of rationality to government.

The corruption and cronyism of the Tammany Hall era was real. LeRoy Harlow, city manager of Daytona Beach, Florida in the early 1950s (well past the advent of the reform movement) struggled to get the city's garbage collection budget under control. He discovered the payroll was inflated by a revolving door of temporary employees, which in turn was due to a variant of the spoils system:

> ...when a worker got on at city yards, he was given a numbered brass disc about the size of a quarter. The workman showed this to a grocer as evidence that he was working for the city, and the grocer would let him buy on credit. When he went off the payroll, he turned in the disc at city yards, and the disc was then given to the worker who replaced him. The significance of the brass disc system was that the employees were told which grocery to buy from, and the grocer rebated a percentage to the city yards bosses...the larger the number of employees with

---

[5]Brad Leonard, Joe Cook, and Jane McNeil, "The Role of Budget and Financial Reform in Making Government Work Better and Cost Less." *Public Budgeting &Finance* (Spring 1995), 12-13.

credit at the store, the larger the total sales...and the larger the kickback to the yard bosses.[6]

As a first step in cleaning up this corrupt system, Harlow fired the refuse superintendent. In response, the public works employees went on strike. Harlow pleaded with them to return to work, and convinced them to take a vote on ending the strike. But as they approached the counter set up in the public works yard, not a single one voted to end the strike. A worker told Harlow what was happening:

> "You know why the men aren't voting?" he asked.
> "No, why?"
> "Because that guy standing by Cliff [the fired refuse superintendent] has an open knife. When a man steps up to the counter, there's a knife blade pressing against his back."[7]

This incident puts the phrase "budget cuts" in a different light! In his book, *Without Fear or Favor*, Harlow further describes the budgeting problems he faced when he arrived at Daytona Beach: little or no citizen involvement in the process, an undefined process for making decisions, requests for city funds from powerful community groups, and unrealistic revenue estimates, among others.[8]

Contrast this with the City of Phoenix, Arizona in more recent times. In the late 1980s, a recession triggered by the

---

[6]LeRoy F. Harlow, *Without Fear or Favor* (Brigham Young University Press, Provo, Utah 1977), 263.
[7]Ibid, 270.
[8]Ibid, 226-315.

collapse of the savings and loan industry caused a drop in the city's property and sales tax revenues. The city manager and staff prepared a detailed list of all city services and programs that were funded through general tax revenues. The city council then collectively assigned priorities to the elements on this list. With this policy direction, the staff then prepared a budget that would match expenditures to the (reduced) revenues, and still maintain critical public services as defined by the elected representatives of the people.

We now see this as the way it *should* be. In America (and much of the rest of the world), we take it for granted that professional staff will spend public dollars efficiently and effectively, in line with the policy direction set by the people through their elected leaders. The budgeting practices that emerged from the reform movement have laid the foundation that supports this expectation.

From a purely *financial* management perspective, there is much to be said for centralized budget control systems, and little to criticize. If public organizations were inanimate black boxes, with revenues as inputs and expenditures as outputs, it would be hard to devise a better system. The CEO (or chief financial officer) is the CPU that keeps the rest of the machine operating efficiently, coordinating and regulating the performance of the various components of the machine. This CPU sends out instructions (the budget manual), and receives feedback in the form of budget requests, and policy inputs from the governing board. Using a set of algorithms, the CPU optimizes the budget, which in turn regulates the amount of resources consumed by the rest of the organization.

But government organizations are not black boxes. In fact, the very concept of an organization (along with revenues, expenditures, and money itself) is an abstraction. In reality, government organizations are just groups of human beings. These human beings spend some of their time and energy to help other people, and other people spend some of their time and energy to keep the government workers fed and housed.

The question then becomes, do current budget practices fit with what we now know about human beings?

3

ARE EMPLOYEES LAZY AND STUPID...OR SOMETHING ELSE?

Ivan Pavlov was awarded the Nobel Prize in 1904 for his work on "reflexive conditioning." He is remembered today for his observation that dogs ("Pavlov's dogs") would salivate automatically (by reflex) when stimulated by something merely *associated* with food, such as the ringing of a bell. In that same year, BF Skinner was born. He would later be the leading figure in behavioral psychology, arguing (among other things) that positive reinforcement can be a powerful influence in human behavior.

Around the same time (the end of the 19th century), Frederick Winslow Taylor, a mechanical engineer, began to lay the foundation for the concept of "scientific management." Work processes (especially industrial production), he urged, could be broken down into their component parts, and managers could analyze the most efficient steps necessary to get a job done. It was then the function of the manager to provide "Detailed instruction and supervision of each worker in the performance of that worker's discrete task."[9] Once given the appropriate detailed direction, the worker would be motivated by being *rewarded* (paid more) as the number of units produced increased.

Scientific management was refined through the introduction of the ideas of time-and-motion studies, standardization, Gantt charts, and efficiency studies. These have had a profound effect on our modern prosperity. Even if human beings are more than cogs in the machine, there is no reason to believe that humans will naturally come together in a work setting and do something useful. In fact, it is easy to imagine a number of activities (drinking beer, dancing, having sex, playing poker, singing) that people would rather do than shoveling coal or pulling a lever on a factory machine. Taylor was correct in observing that there must be something added to the equation to motivate and direct individuals so that their collective effort (which often involves a very large collection of individuals) actually produces a desired outcome.

Standardization and efficient work processes led, of course, to the success of mass production of everything from cars to airplanes. As more of this work is being done by robots (which have not, as yet, evolved to the point of true artificial intelligence), then "Detailed instruction and supervision of each worker [robot] in the performance of that worker's discrete task" is probably the best way to make widgets.

---

[9]David Montgomery, *The Fall of the House of Labor: The Workplace, the State, and American Labor Activism* (Cambridge University Press, 1989), 250.

Taylor's work provided a quantum leap forward in improved efficiency, but it turns out it was less than optimal because Taylor and other supporters of scientific management grossly underestimated human potential. In a nutshell, they believed people were inherently lazy and stupid. Frederick Taylor told a congressional committee:

> I can say, without the slightest hesitationthat the science of handling pig-iron is so great that the man who is ... physically able to handle pig-iron and is sufficiently phlegmatic and stupid to choose this for his occupation is rarely able to comprehend the science of handling pig-iron.[10]

Taylor elaborated a general rule: "This inability of the man who is fit to do the work to understand the science of doing his work becomes more and more evident, as the work becomes more complicated, all the way up the scale. [The] law is almost universal...that the man who is fit to work at any particular trade is unable to understand the science of that trade without kindly help and cooperation of men of a totally different kind of education..."[11]

Even at the time, however, Taylor's ideas were challenged. Some took issue with his assertion that there was "one best way" to do a job. Others were uncomfortable with his characterization of workers. Robert Kanigel writes,

---

[10]Ibid, 251.Montgomery's source: *U.S Congress, House of Representatives, Hearings before the Special Committee of the House of Representatives to Investigate the Taylor and Other Systems of Shop Management* (Washington DC, 1911), 1397.
[11]Ibid, 251.

Scientific management was degrading. In reducing work to instructions and rules, it took away your knowledge and skill. In standing over you with a stopwatch, peering at you, measuring you, rating you, it treated you like a side of beef. You weren't supposed to think. Whatever workmanly pride you might once have possessed must be sacrificed on the altar of efficiency, your role only to execute the will of other men paid to think for you. You were a drone, fit only for taking orders. Scientific management, then, worked people with scant regard not only for the limitations of their bodies but for the capacities of their minds."[12]

Even if Taylor himself had opponents and challengers, the idea of centralized, top-down control of decisions and work processes was never really challenged. A hierarchical structure of power and control is as old as human civilization itself.[13]

Theory X and Theory Y.

A half century after the dawn of scientific management, Douglas McGregor published *The Human Side of Enterprise.* He labeled the traditional view of workers and how they should

---

[12] Robert Kanigel, *The One Best Way: Fredrick Winslow Taylor and the Enigma of Efficiency* (New York: Penguin Books), 1997. As quoted in Wagner & Harter, *12: The Elements of Great Managing* (New York: Gallup Press 2006), 98-99.
[13] Even Moses struggled with the concept of delegation of authority (*Exodus 18*).

be managed as "Theory X." McGregor's description of the assumptions of Theory X fit well with Taylorism:

1. The average human being has an inherent dislike of work and will avoid it if he can.
2. Most people must be coerced, controlled, directed, threatened with punishment to get them to put forth adequate effort toward the achievement of organizational objectives.
3. The average human being prefers to be directed, wishes to avoid responsibility, has relatively little ambition, wants security above all.[14]

McGregor didn't assert that these assumptions were wrong, but he wondered if they were accurate. Abraham Maslow had proposed that "self-actualization" is in fact a stronger motivator than the "hygiene" issues of security and adequate pay. Maslow's *A Theory of Human Motivation* was published in Psychological Review in 1943, followed by his book, *Motivation and Personality* in 1954.

Building on this and similar work, McGregor proposed a different way of viewing workers and their motivation. The assumptions underlying his "Theory Y" are:

- The expenditure of physical and mental effort in work is as natural as play or rest.
- External control and the threat of punishment are not the only means for bringing about effort toward organizational objectives. Man will exercise self-

---

[14] Douglas McGregor, *The Human Side of Enterprise* (McGraw-Hill, 1960), 33-34.

direction and self-control in the service of objective to which he is committed.

- Commitment to objectives is a function of the rewards associated with their achievement.
- The average human being learns, under proper conditions not only to accept but to seek responsibility.
- The capacity to exercise a relatively high degree of imagination, ingenuity, and creativity in the solution of organizational problems is widely, not narrowly, distributed in the population.
- Under the conditions of modern industrial life, the intellectual potentialities of the average human being are only partially utilized.[15]

Note that Theory Y does not challenge (or for that matter, address) the aspects of "scientific management" that focus on process improvements or increased efficiency. The organizational objectives of Theory Y can certainly include improved quality or reduced operating costs. The difference between Theory X and Theory Y is in the approach to attaining these objectives. Under Theory X the manager identifies and directs all process improvements, and the employee obediently carries them out. Under Theory Y, process improvements are a *joint effort* of managers and line employees. The very act of devising better methods of getting work done can be rewarding in and of itself.

Rather than a philosophy in which managers direct and control subordinates, Theory Y emphasizes the importance

---

of *self-control*, in which each employee is both accountable and responsible for his or her own performance. And if managers should respect and act on this philosophy, then so too should staff functions such as personnel, finance, and budget. McGregor notes:

> The central principle of managerial control is the principle of self-control. This principle severely limits *both* staff and line use of data and information collected for control purposes as well as the so-called coordinative activities of staff groups. If the principle of self-control is violated, the staff inevitably becomes involved in conflicting obligations, and in addition is required to occupy the incompatible roles of professional helper and policeman.[16]

As Douglas McGregor was writing *The Human Side of Enterprise*, Frederick Herzberg was summarizing the results of his psychological research in *The Motivation to Work*. He found that, while employees could be de-motivated by "hygiene" factors such as low pay or bad working conditions, they are largely motivated by achievement, recognition, responsibility, advancement, and work itself. This is of course counter to Taylor's belief that employees tend to be lazy and stupid, and are motivated only by the possibility of more pay under a piece-work system.

Herzberg followed this book, a few years later, with his famous Harvard Business Review article, *One More Time: How Do You Motivate Employees?* A key to job satisfaction is job

---

[16]Ibid, 173.

enrichment, including such things as:

a. Removing some controls while retaining accountability
b. Increasing the accountability of individuals for own work
c. Giving a person a complete natural unit of work
d. Granting additional authority to an employee in his or her activity; job freedom
e. Making periodic reports directly available to the worker rather than to the supervisor
f. Introducing new and more difficult tasks not previously handled
g. Assigning individuals specific or specialized tasks, enabling them to become experts[17]

A common thread in McGregor's and Herzberg's work is the idea that employees like having control over their jobs, and in how they approach their work. They are not mere cogs in a machine; a job well-done is a reward in itself, and people need the tools and resources (and permission) that enable them to do good work. Herzberg specifically notes the importance of control of resources—"mini-budgets, tools, etc. necessary to do the job"—as a positive factor in motivation.[18]

While a half century has passed since the publication of *The Human Side of Enterprise*, management scholars have

---

[17] Frederick Herzberg, "One More Time: How Do You Motivate Employees?" *Harvard Business Review*, 46 No. 1 (Jan/Feb 1968), 59.
[18] Frederick Herzberg, *The Motivation to Work* (New Brunswick: Transaction Publishers (2007), xv. Initially published in 1959.

confirmed that the assumptions of Theory Y are generally correct, and that following a Theory X approach to management, in which employees are assumed to be lazy and stupid and the manager needs to direct their work, is generally bad for an organization. Peter Drucker notes (in a collection of his writings published in 2001):

> Self-control means stronger motivation: a desire to do the best rather than just enough to get by. It means higher performance goals and broader vision...That management by self-control is highly desirable will hardly be disputed in America or in American business today. Its acceptance underlies all the talk of "pushing decisions down to the lowest possible level," or of "paying people for results." But to make management by self-control a reality requires more than acceptance of the concept as right and desirable. It requires new tools and far-reaching changes in traditional thinking and practices...Each manager should have the information he needs to measure his own performance and should receive it soon enough to make any changes necessary for the desired results. And this information should go to the manager himself, and not to his superior. It should be the means of self-control, not a tool of control from above.[19]

Drucker acknowledges that individuals are wired differently, and good supervisors recognize this and manage

---

[19] Peter Drucker, *The Essential Drucker* (Harper Collins 2001), 120-121.

accordingly.[20] But he observes that,

> The productivity of the knowledge worker is likely to
> become the center of the management of people, just
> as the work on the productivity of the manual worker
> became the center of managing people a hundred
> years ago, that is, since Frederick W. Taylor. This will
> require, above all, very different assumptions about
> people in organizations and their work: One does not
> "manage" people. The task is to lead people. And the
> goal is to make productive the specific strengths and
> knowledge of each individual.[21]

Tom Peters, in *Thriving on Chaos* (1987), emphasizes the
importance of empowering managers and staff, and that the
individual's control over resources (budget and spending) is a
critical means of empowerment:

> Increased spending authority does not entail a loss of
> control. To the contrary, it begets more control of the
> most powerful sort—self-control. Low spending
> control leads to shenanigans—avoid a $1,000 limit by
> making an endless stream of $999.95 requisitions.
> High spending authority says to the worker, or unit
> boss, "I take you seriously." The monkey is on his or
> her back to live up to the trust.[22]

---

[20] Gerald Seijts, Gary Latham, Kevin Tasa& Brandon Latham, "Goal
Setting and Goal Orientation: An Integration of Two Different Yet
Related Literatures," *Academy of Management Journal,* 47 No. 2
(2004), 227-239.
[21] Drucker, 80-81.
[22] Tom Peters, *Thriving on Chaos* (Harper Collins, 1991), 614.

The results of research have consistently supported the importance of giving staff the tools they need to do the job. The Gallup Organization, over twenty-five years, conducted over 80,000 interviews with managers and employees of over 400 organizations. They found that employees both get the greatest job satisfaction, and do their best work, when twelve conditions are satisfied. One of them is, "Do I have the materials and equipment I need to do my work right?"[23] For managers, "materials and equipment" are ultimately represented by budget authority.

---

[23] Marcus Buckingham & Curt Coffman, *First, Break All the Rules: What the World's Greatest Managers Do Differently* (Simon & Schuster, 1999).

SCOTT DOUGLAS LAZENBY

4

THEORY X AND TRADITIONAL BUDGET PROCESSES

Budget practices that emerged a hundred years ago, concurrent with the concepts of "scientific management," were consistent with Taylorism. The upper levels of the organization needed to control both the work practices of employees, and their access to and use of organizational resources. A 1937 paper on "The Beginnings of Business Budgeting" noted that the standardization prescribed by scientific management provided a tool for the CEO or controller to set budget amounts:

> Production costs were for a long time not computable, except in a general way. It was not until Taylor attempted to standardize production operations, by time studies and test runs, that production costs could be accurately computed... Taylor and his immediate followers thus supplied a measuring technique that is being applied with equal

effectiveness to all other operations of a business, as well as production, by means of *budgetary procedure.* Sound methods of standardization are an essential prerequisite for *budgetary control.*[24] (Emphasis added.)

City managers were quick to adopt corporate budget practices as a tool for administrative control. Leonard White, writing in 1927, notes:

> The [city] managers have consistently been convinced advocates of the budget...They have taken their financial duties with great seriousness and on the whole have displayed qualities of sound, if not brilliant, financiering. By this is meant that they have drafted conservative estimates of revenue and expenditure and have remained within their appropriations, avoiding deficits except in emergency cases...Perhaps no achievement stands out so clearly in the survey which is the basis of this book as the uniform care in the use of public money. In bringing about this result, the managers have applied modern methods. They receive full statements monthly and quarterly, cumulated so that they know the situation of each department and each account...They are insistent that each department live within its appropriation.

Just as central, top-down control of work processes was a key feature of Taylorism and scientific management, central

---

[24] Edwin L. Theiss, "The Beginnings of Business Budgeting." *The Accounting Review*, 12, No. 1 (Mar., 1937), 48.

control of spending was a key feature of budgeting in the reform era:

> At the outset, the budget was viewed as an instrument of control...These early budgets were, and for the most part still are, authorizations to spend-appropriations-for particular "objects of expenditure" such as personal services, commodities, travel, and the like. The appropriation was the "upper limit" much like a thermal control on a furnace: when the limit is reached the fuel, or, in the fiscal sense, the money is stopped. The upper limit was imposed through the approving of the budget by the governing body-the board, the council, the legislature, etc.[25]

Thus, the primary function of an adopted budget is one of control: limiting the spending of operating managers since, presumably, without this control managers would spend more than the organization could afford, and spend money on the wrong things. This fits well with a Theory X view of employees (they prefer to be directed, and wish to avoid responsibility). Leonard White notes, "Managers have found in the smaller cities that they cannot depend upon the financial judgment of their department heads. [Ossian] Carr [city manager of Dubuque, Iowa and Fort Worth, Texas, among others] declares their estimates to be worthless, and generally the managers rely heavily on their judgment in preference to the judgment of their subordinates." p.248

But it isn't only the final product (the adopted budget)

[25] Selwyn Becker & David Green, Jr., "Budgeting and Employee Behavior," *The Journal of Business*, 35, No. 4 (Oct., 1962), 392

and how it is managed that reflects a Theory X philosophy. The very process of adopting a budget reflects the same philosophy. Let's revisit the typical budget cycle described in Chapter 2.

Budget instructions.

Revenues are collected centrally, and only the central management and finance staff can see the big picture that describes the overall financial condition of the organization. They also retain control over projections of future revenues. Therefore, operating managers must be instructed on how to prepare their own budgets.

Budget requests.

Here, lip service is given to the operating managers' knowledge and understanding of their own programs and services. The budget "request" is the way they *participate* in the budget process. But it's a zero-sum game, in which each department competes with the other for a limited pot of money. And the game is ruled by the CEO or budget director: the operating manager proposes, but the CEO (and ultimately the governing board) disposes. It is at this stage that so many of the "shenanigans" (to use Tom Peters' phrase) occur. This "us versus them" mentality reinforces the idea that central management must ride herd on the free-spending, undisciplined and ignorant departments.

Budget hearings and decisions.

Once the budget request leaves the department, the CEO and board are left to do the hard work of balancing the budget (since, after all, employees prefer to be directed and want to avoid responsibility). In larger bureaucracies, budget analysts (or "budgeteers") add another staff layer between the operating manager and CEO, sometimes advocating for the department, but often exerting control by exposing the budget shenanigans that the budget request process encourages and otherwise questioning the department's intelligence, competence, and honesty.

Games People Play

Budget games and shenanigans are a direct result of the rules of the game; they do not reflect personality defects of the players in the game. Budget and finance staff will roll their eyes and shake their heads at these games, but the behavior they condemn is a completely predicable and natural result of a centralized, top-down budget system. Experienced operating managers who are skilled at playing the game (i.e., by not getting caught) are admired not only by their own employees and by their competitors (other departments), but also (grudgingly) by the central referees of the game.

The following list of twenty-one budget tricks is based on over three decades of professional experience on both sides of the playing field. A Theory X approach to management encourages these tricks, and also provides some antidotes.

1. Magic disappearing revenue. The budget just won't balance, but you don't want to cut spending. Just increase the revenue estimate to make it balance...and worry about it later. <u>Management response</u>: Account for all revenues centrally, and have central finance staff perform all revenue estimates and projections.

2. The sacrificial lamb. The budget office asks for a list of programs that could be cut if spending reductions are necessary. The department head offers up the pet programs of the CEO or governing body (e.g., army base closures), knowing they will be held sacred. This is the oldest trick in the book, yet people keep doing it. (This trick is also known as the Washington Monument Syndrome: if the National Park Service is told to reduce its budget, the first thing it will propose to cut is operation of the popular Washington Monument).

Management response: When the tactic is too blatant, discipline the offending manager.

3. Groundhog Day. The police chief requests an additional traffic enforcement officer, promising that additional traffic tickets will pay for the position. Over the next few years, the position is shifted to other areas, and traffic enforcement drops off. The chief then requests an additional patrol officer, promising that additional traffic tickets will pay for the position.

Management response: Keep careful records during budget hearings in order to expose this trick and deny the request.

4. It's only routine replacement. The parks department scrounges some old surplus conference chairs and a table from another department. In the next budget cycle they include a request to replace the aging office equipment.

Management response: Create new rules allowing for replacement costs only when equipment was originally purchased through an approved budget line item.

5. Grants? What grants? The department adds a plug in the budget in case a grant is received. The grant application is unsuccessful, but the spending authority remains in the budget (and the money gets spent).

Management response: Centralize both revenues *and* expenditure budgets for grant-funded programs, to ensure that departments do not have access to the funds until the grant is secured.

6. Spend it or lose it. Another old trick, with many variants. The department has a goal of spending every penny in the budget, both to avoid losing it at the end of the fiscal year, and to prove to the pesky budget analysts that they really need every cent in their budget.

Management response: Institute an arbitrary (and unpredictable) cutoff date for requisitions, to catch departments off guard. Or provide extra scrutiny of requisitions near the end of the fiscal year, demanding thorough justification for each dollar spent.

7. Don't ask, it's technical. The public works director slips in a request for a new riding lawn mower (for park maintenance), sandwiched between a twenty million dollar water plant upgrade and a ten million dollar sewer plant expansion. The city council members spend most of the budget hearing talking about their personal experience with lawn mowers, and gloss over the treatment plant budgets.

Management response: Allow the governing body to see only the total cost of the program; let the professionals (central staff) deal with the details since they are too sophisticated to be tricked like this.

8. The myth of the "current services" budget. The department increases next year's budget by a combination of inflation and population growth, conveniently ignoring economies of scale, substitution of different goods and services, and the fact that not all costs follow the Consumer Price Index.

Management response: Entrust central department staff with the task of constructing complex forecasting models to ascertain the "true" cost increase.

9. The moving target. Major capital improvement projects (e.g., roads, buildings) are done over several years. Few budget systems track total spending versus the original budget over multiple years, making it easy for the manager to hide the true cost of the project.

Management response: Establish central multi-year tracking systems for capital improvements, and give project managers an annual allotment, making sure the allotment for the final year guarantees the project will remain within the original budget.

10. Spending the savings. New equipment is requested in the budget on the basis of future operating savings. Somehow the manager forgets to request a smaller budget in future years.

Management response: Keep careful notes during the budget process, and cut the department's budget in the future when the promised savings are supposed to occur.

11. Going to the well. A senior employee retires, yielding an unexpected windfall in salary savings that the department manager shifts somewhere else. But when the air conditioning system goes out, she asks the Board of Commissioners for a transfer from the general fund contingency account.

Management response: Assign the central budget analyst the task of poring over the department's budget to see if the air conditioner can be purchased out of savings, and to verify the accuracy of the department's estimate of the cost of the air conditioner.

12. If it saves just one life. This simple phrase has been used to justify all sorts of dubious spending on equipment and personnel by fire departments and other public safety agencies.

Management response: When the fire chief says, "you can't put a price on a life," bring in an actuary to point out that, yes, you can.

13. The old switcheroo. The department manager argues hard (and successfully) for the expensive piece of equipment they must have to do the job properly. When the ink is dry on the final budget, the manager buys the cheaper item that he knew all along would work, and spends the savings somewhere else.

Management response: Budget for the (expensive) equipment in a separate line item, and prohibit any savings from being spent elsewhere.

14. Look what we found. In a variation of #13, the department gets budget approval to replace the motor pool car. They discover that they can, in fact, keep the old car running another year, and spend the appropriation elsewhere. Next year they request funds to replace the pool car.

Management response: Keep careful notes during the budget process, and discipline the department manager when this trick is used (the employee's annual performance review, nine months later, would be a good time to do this).

15. Poor me. The department makes a show of its run-down equipment and office furniture, to prove to policy makers how under-funded it is.

Management response: Criticize the department for not taking better care of its equipment.

16. The nose under the tent. The manager budgets for a new position, starting in the last quarter of the fiscal year. The salary and fringe cost seems modest enough, but the full impact is hidden until the next fiscal year, at which time the program is up and running with a new group of clients.

Management response: This is just the cost of doing business.

17. The gift that keeps on giving. The police chief argues successfully for a new officer. The budget includes recurring salary and operating costs, and one-time costs for a car and radios. The one-time costs are magically rolled into the regular budget request the next year.

Management response: Keep careful notes during the budget process, and reduce next year's budget by the cost of the car and radios.

18. The accountants made me do it. Line items with obscure or unusual names (merchant fees, ODEQ regulatory fees) are padded, knowing that the simple ones (travel, office supplies) are the only ones that will be attacked.

Management response: Hire central budget analysts to examine the use of these line items, and challenge department's budget estimates.

19. Whoops, where did it go? A new program is proposed that will be supported by user fees. Near the end of the process, the manager "sacrifices" the program for a smaller expenditure (except that the smaller program generates no user fees).

Management response: Again, hire central budget analysts to keep on top of issues like this.

20. The long sunset. A five-year lease purchase payment ends. Strangely, the amount stays in the budget for several more years.

Management response: Maintain a large and detailed central tickler file to remind central budget managers when departmental budget items are no longer justified.

21. If it's the private sector, it must be efficient. High salaries and expensive equipment are hidden in a lump sum private contract payment; no one can see the line items.

Management response: Insist on cost-plus contracts, where the agency must review and approve the line item expenses of the contractor.

This list is, of course, overly simplistic. In the real us versus them budget game, these tricks are only Round One. The vigilant central budget director and the resourceful operating manager each have a bag full of weapons at their disposal as they thrust and parry in the ongoing game. To counter the "spend it or lose it" behavior, the budget director sets an arbitrary cutoff date for requisitions. So the next year, the operating manager simply spends sooner. The budget director counters by assigning analysts to scrutinize all requisitions. The operating manager counters by overwhelming the analyst with a flood of requisitions for essential supplies. The budget director counters by simply sitting on the requisitions. The operating manager counters by using a credit card and on-line purchases to bypass the requisition process entirely. The budget director counters by getting the finance director to complain to the CEO on the egregious violation of purchasing protocols. The operating manager counters by putting equipment on lease-purchase agreements, and entering into multi-year contracts for services so the organization has no choice over paying. The budget director counters by insisting on review and approval of all contracts and lease agreements. The operating manager counters by withholding service from citizens, blaming the budget director when the citizens protest. The budget director counters by complaining to the CEO. The operating manager counters by quietly urging the citizens to go to the governing board. In the next budget cycle, the governing board approves a modest and symbolic increase in the department's budget, and the game starts over.

The paradox here is that traditional Theory X budget rules assume that the operating managers, who are too lazy and stupid to run their own departments without central oversight, are in fact very smart, energetic, and resourceful when playing the budget game.

5

TOWARD A THEORY Y APPROACH TO BUDGETING

The work of McGregor, Maslow, Herzberg, Likert and others was not lost on government managers. For many, the principles of Theory Y resonated with their own observations and beliefs about people. They adopted an empowering and encouraging attitude in personal interactions with their employees. They delegated meaningful work to their mid-managers, and tried to avoid micro-managing. When asked about their management "style" in job interviews, they professed their earnest belief that line employees are in the best position to suggest process improvements, that the manager's job is to support the good work of the line employees, and that good managers are leaders, not administrators.

But while these managers used Theory Y language, it was lip service only because their organization's systems, procedures, and rules continued to be based on the old Theory X assumptions.

One city manager, proudly describing how she had brought more empowerment and participation to her organization, pointed out that she had changed the criteria for their annual performance reviews to include elements of their new participatory philosophy, so that employees would be praised for behaviors like working well with teammates, and to cooperate with people in other departments. Job descriptions were revised to include the new participatory values. A pay for performance system rewarded initiative and teamwork. Employees were given resources to work more independently, such as training in how the purchasing system worked. Management negotiated with the union on the implications of the changes.

The irony here is the very tools she was using—annual performance reviews, static job descriptions, pay-for-performance schemes, centralized purchasing, and adversarial union contracts—are very much Theory X tools, established precisely to keep lazy and stupid employees in check. It is easy to imagine the excuse given for the lack of results of the new management style of participation and empowerment: "We encouraged the HR department to submit a budget request for training mid managers in participatory management, but unfortunately finances were tight and it didn't make it through the budget process."

Ken Miller, in *Extreme Government Makeover,* makes an eloquent case that the problem with dysfunctional government isn't the *people* who work in the government, but the *systems* that the government creates to provide services and regulation.[26] He uses the metaphor of the plumbing in a house to describe these processes and systems:

> The systems of government—the pipes—are a mess. They're kinked up by decades of specialization, reorganizations, cover-your-ass (CYA) efforts, cost-cutting, and abandoned technology projects. They've been outsourced, in-sourced, downsized, right-sized, and zero-based budgeted. And now they're so twisted and slow, they make a silly straw look efficient.[27]

A new management philosophy or management "style" won't make any difference in an organization with the same old plumbing. Most governments—and large private bureaucracies, for that matter—are governed by rules and systems that assume employees are lazy and stupid, and those rules will determine employee behavior, regardless of the degree of enlightenment of the CEO or key department heads.

This isn't the place for a comprehensive review of all the Theory X systems that are woven into our organizations. The point is that while many managers understand the shortcomings of Theory X (i.e., it is based on erroneous assumptions about human nature), adopting a Theory Y "philosophy" is only a partial solution when the very systems and processes that are embedded in their organizations keep them in a Theory X world. Budget systems are a good place to start in a process of organizational reform.

---

[26] Ken Miller, *Extreme Government Makeover: Increasing Our Capacity to Do More Good* (Governing Books, 2011).
[27] Ibid., Kindle Location 273.

Some government managers (still a very small minority) are doing this. In *Reinventing Government,* published two decades ago, Ted Gaebler and David Osborne describe a new approach to budgeting called "Expenditure Control Budgeting." They note a pernicious problem in government: "our budget systems actually encourage every public manager to waste money."[28] In 1979, the City of Fairfield, California, found a solution to this problem.

> As is so often the case, [the solution] sprang from the mind of an outsider, who was unencumbered by the knowledge that "it's always been done this way." Fairfield's assistant finance director was an immigrant from the Philippines, where he had been a banker. He could not believe how Fairfield budgeted. He suggested to City Manager Gale Wilson that Fairfield budget the way his bank did in the Philippines, roughly the way a family budgets: it sets up accounts for various major expenditures, but if something breaks down or an opportunity comes along, it shifts money from one account to another.[29]

The system adopted by Fairfield, (and soon thereafter by city manager Ted Gaebler in Visalia) had these features:

- Managers are responsible for the bottom line, not individual line items. They are free to shift amounts between line items to achieve the organization's goals.

---

[28] Ted Gaebler & David Osborne, *Reinventing Government* (Addison-Wesley, Reading MA, 1992), 119
[29] Ibid., 119.

- The bottom line includes any revenues that can be attributed to the department. So if they find a way to bring in more revenue, they can spend more. Conversely, if their revenue projections are overly optimistic, the burden is on them to adjust spending.
- Budget savings (or at least some significant percentage of them) can be carried over into the next fiscal year.
- Rather than having departments compete in a free-for-all for resources in a budget request process, operating managers are instead given budget targets. The targets were initially set by formula, but could be adjusted by the city manager.

In spite of its name, Expenditure Control Budgeting (we can refer to it as ECB, in the tradition of budget theory that favors initials like ZBB and PPBS) is actually about *giving up* control over budget decisions. ECB can only be instituted by the chief executive officer and/or budget director, and they are the ones that give up control and transfer it to the operating managers. They empower their managers, and the only way to do it is to weaken their own power (or at least appear to; more on this later). Osborne and Gaebler admit that the "Expenditure Control Budgeting" label was a marketing gimmick, designed to mollify city councils and others who assumed that operating managers were conniving bastards who couldn't be trusted with money.[30]

Other cities in the southwest tried the approach, liked it, and adopted as a permanent element of their internal systems.

---

[30]Ibid., 120.

One such city was Chandler, Arizona, a suburb of Phoenix. The city's operating management policies include the statement, "Department Heads are expected to manage their areas with the overall financial health of the City in mind. With Expenditure Control Budgeting (ECB) 'Managers are paid to manage' and to look for effective and efficient ways to deliver quality services to our citizens while meeting Council goals."

Chandler's budget document describes ECB this way:

> In order to encourage cost effectiveness while providing quality services to Chandler citizens, Expenditure Control Budgeting (ECB) is used for General Fund cost centers. Under the ECB philosophy, any savings accumulated in the operating accounts are carried forward within the cost centers to the next year. Department directors have the ability to expend accumulated savings toward any type of City-approved expenditure except for personnel services. Departments are allowed to control their own operations and maintenance (O&M) expenditures by developing their own line item budgets. Department directors are allowed flexibility in programming and allocating funds within their own O&M budgets.[31]

In Chandler, carryover savings are limited to savings in non-personnel budgets. An argument for doing this is that once a department has the authorization for a position, the

---

[31]City of Chandler, AZ budget accessed at
http://www.chandleraz.gov/default.aspx?pageid=34.

operating manager has very little control over pay and benefit costs. Wages are often set by union contracts (usually negotiated city-wide), and organization-wide cost-of-living increases are typically set by the governing board. Pension and medical/dental benefit costs are also (typically) set centrally, outside the control of the managers of the operating departments.

The use of ECB supports the following basic beliefs:

- Department directors and supervisors are paid to manage wisely and to look for effective and efficient ways to deliver quality services to our citizens while meeting the goals of Council;
- Department directors and supervisors can find more ways to do things more efficiently if given the freedom to innovate and control their own resources; and
- Budgeting is a means to an end, not an end in itself.[32]

Other local governments have experimented with elements of Expenditure Control Budgeting; they include Dade County, FL and Westminster, CO[33]; Glendale, AZ; and Medford and Sandy, OR. [34]

The process of reforming internal systems is more challenging at the state government level, due to the complexity and size of the state organizations. Elements of ECB have, however, been tested in subunits of state

---

[32]Ibid., p. 45 of budget document.
[33]Dan Cothran, "Entrepreneurial Budgeting: An Emerging Reform?" *Public Administration Review*, 53, No. 5 (Sep.-Oct., 1995), 445-454
[34]Author's personal experience.

government, including the San Diego campus of the University of California[35] and the Vancouver campus of Washington State University.[36]

In the late 1980s, the State of Minnesota faced a number of the challenges that plague bureaucracies in which staff functions begin to dominate line functions. Michael Barzelay describes several horror stories that sound all too familiar to operating managers in government.[37] As just one example, a community college needed 50 personal computers for a new course on using computers. In spite of the fact that the requisition was submitted well in advance, as the first day of class approached, the computers had still not arrived. The central purchasing department explained that, in order to get the maximum effect from volume purchasing, all PC orders were being combined for a single bidding process later in the year. The college was forced to cancel the class.

The Governor and top staff initiated a number of changes centered around the concept that staff agencies support the (service-providing) line agencies, not the other way around. Internal functions of information technology, human resources, fleet management, legal services, and purchasing were realigned to treat operating departments as customers, sometimes even bidding against outside vendors or other internal departments for the operating department's business. But for some time, financial management— operating in the old philosophy of centralized top-down control—resisted reform. To the relief of the operating

---

[35]Cothran, 447.

[36] Personal conversation with IT Director Gregory Alpernas

[37] Michael Barzelay, *Breaking Through Bureaucracy: A New Vision for Managing in Government* (University of California Press, 1992).

managers, Peter Hutchinson, the new commissioner of finance, embraced the direction the state organization was taking.

Hutchinson describes his experience in *The Price of Government*, co-authored with David Osborne. The State of Minnesota adopted the key elements of Expenditure Control Budgeting. Operating managers were given base budgets (the "price" the taxpayers were willing to pay for the service) and were then challenged to maximize the *outcomes* of their operations. They were given freedom to increase the quantity and quality of the services they provided in a number of ways, including contracting with other agencies or private providers for service provision.

If most state governments are deeply entrenched in Theory X systems, change comes even slower in the national government. The report of the National Performance Review, led in 1993 by Vice President Al Gore, noted that

> Solutions to these problems [arbitrary restrictions on moving resources, year end spending sprees] exist. They have been tested in local governments, in state governments, even in the federal government. Essentially, they involve budget systems with fewer line items, more authority for managers to move money among line items, and freedom for agencies to keep some or all of what they save—thus minimizing the incentive for year-end spending sprees.[38]

---

[38]Vice President Al Gore, *From Red Tape to Results: Creating a Government That Works Better and Costs Less*, (Washington: Government Printing Office, 1993), 18.

Specific recommendations from the National Performance Review include a biennial budget process, increased flexibility in spending by reducing the number of individual line item appropriations and budget allotments, a reduction in overlapping restrictions (i.e., limits on both spending and the number of authorized staff members), and allowing operating managers to carry over half their budget savings.

Predictably, many of these proposed reforms were not implemented (see Chapter 8). But they were vigorously debated, even if the proposed changes in the budget system were eclipsed by some of the other elements of the National Performance Review report (entrepreneurial management and privatization, to name a few).

And in any case, Vice President Gore was correct: Expenditure Control Budgeting *has* been tested in local governments as well as in some state governments. Some cities have had three decades of experience with it: plenty of time for trial-and-error, feedback, and fine-tuning. The concepts are well beyond the experimental stage.

6

THEORY Y BUDGETING IN PRACTICE

The previous chapter introduced the concept of "Expenditure Control Budgeting" as initially introduced in Fairfield, California. Here the term "Theory Y Budgeting" will be used as a more general label for a variety of budget-related processes and systems that are consistent with the research on human behavior conducted by McGregor, Herzberg, and others. It includes all of the elements of ECB as well as other systems and processes that relate to the budget and that support a philosophy of empowering operating managers and employees.

The intent is to provide fairly generic prescriptions for a Theory Y budget process that can be applied to governments of any level or type. To illustrate the concepts, examples are drawn from the author's own experience in several local governments (of varying sizes and in different states). But those examples are for illustration only; the specifics can be adapted to meet the needs of the organization.

Start With Why

For many accountants and budget analysts, the budget process begins with the budget manual, or the instructions to departments and managers on how to prepare the budget for the next fiscal cycle. It should, in fact, begin much earlier than this. Whether or not a formal part of the process, the budget development exercise begins with input from the "owners" of the organization: the government's citizens.

In a Theory Y budget process, this is an absolutely critical component, not only because it reflects good government, but also because it is a powerful source of motivation and direction for operating managers and their staff. Simon Sinek, in *Start With Why*, emphasizes the importance of the role leaders play in instilling a sense of purpose in their organizations.[39] We all want to be a part of something bigger than ourselves, to be engaged in work that has meaning and value.

This holds true for private corporations, even when they are merely selling perfume to make people smell good or a smartphone that people *experience* rather than use. A sense of purpose is (or should be) an even more powerful motivator in governments, which after all exist to make the world (or at least the immediate community) a better place. Many people are drawn to government organizations as a result of their public service values. They are motivated by a desire to make a difference in peoples' lives.

The sense of purpose is strengthened when the staff (as

[39] Simon Sinek, *Start with Why: How Great Leaders Inspire Everyone to Take Action* (Portfolio Trade, 2011)

well as the elected representatives) of the government have a clear sense of the wants and needs of the citizens, and can make a connection between those wants and needs and the work they do. In some areas, the need is obvious. When a firefighter rescues a person in a burning building, there is no doubt about the need, and the purpose of the fire department in meeting that need. But in other areas, more work needs to be done to understand the priorities and desires of residents.

Examples

The City of Sandy has, over the years, used a wide variety of citizen input and engagement techniques. They include surveys in the water bill newsletter, snap polls on the city web site, social media comments, neighborhood meetings and ice cream socials, and focus groups. One of the most effective (although labor-intensive) techniques draws from Peter Block's community-building principles, where the members of the city council act as hosts and conveners for community dialog on challenging issues; these forums use elements of the World Cafe process.[40]

Other governments have tried other tactics. The City of Medford, Oregon, instituted a Neighborhood Walk program, in which city council members and top staff simply went door to door, talking to residents about their needs and concerns, and how the city could help. This, of course, wouldn't be practical for larger cities, or county or state governments, but these

---

[40] Juanita Brown, *The World Cafe: Shaping Our Futures Through Conversations That Matter* (Berrett-Koehler, 2005)

organizations have access to other tools. The point is that some process for understanding citizen priorities and needs to take place.

And there is no need to tie citizen engagement directly to the budget cycle. In fact, the typical scheme for citizen input in the budget process is to lasso a handful of "average citizens" onto a budget committee, and to hold a public hearing when the budget is adopted. These are worse than useless, for several reasons. First, they occur too late in the process to have much influence on it. Second, very few citizens bother to participate this way.[41] And finally, the average citizen is notoriously ignorant of the details of government finance and services,[42] and citizen input on the *means* (rather than the *ends*) of service provision is of little benefit. What citizens *are* good at (when the right techniques are used to draw it out) is supplying the basic values and vision that serve to guide the future of the government.[43] To be effective, this kind of citizen engagement needs to occur well before a budget process formally begins.

Direction from the Governing Board

Direct feedback from citizens is important, but in our representative democracy, so is direction from the elected representatives of the citizens. As with citizen input, strong

[41] Jonathan Walters, "O Citizen Where Art Thou?" *Governing,* April, 2009.
[42] Rick Shenkman, *Just How Stupid Are We?: Facing the Truth About the American Voter* (Basic Books, 2008).
[43] Daniel Yankelovitch, *The Magic of Dialog: Transforming Conflict into Cooperation* (Touchstone, 2001).

leadership by the governing body helps clarify the purpose of the organization, and can be a source of inspiration and motivation for staff. Challenging but achievable goals that are set by the elected leadership of the government provide staff with targets to work toward, and a sense of accomplishment when the goals are met.

In addition to contributing to the organization's sense of purpose, direction from the governing body is a key component in building trust between elected officials and staff. Theory Y budgeting gives operating managers a high degree of administrative discretion; they are given a great deal of flexibility in the use of budget resources to get the job done. For this system to work, it's critical that the services and projects delivered by the operating managers *are the same ones* that the governing board wants done. In other words, there needs to be close alignment between the outcomes desired by the governing board, and the outcomes that the employees of the government are working toward. And for this to happen, the governing board needs to put some effort into articulating its goals.

This may seem obvious, but for a variety of reasons, the practice of goal-setting by the governing board isn't as common as one might think (just go on the Internet and try to find the adopted goals of your local school board). Peter Sellers, in *Dr. Strangelove, or How I Learned to Stop Worrying and Love the Bomb,* utters this marvelous line: "the whole point of a Doomsday Machine is lost, *if you keep it a secret!*" Even if coming to a consensus is a difficult process, the governing board needs to be very clear on its goals and expectations; the point of a governing board as policy leaders of the government is lost if they keep their goals a secret. An attitude of "I can't define it, but I know it when I see it," may work for a Supreme Court grappling with the definition of pornography, but it is useless for the operating managers of a government who are motivated to make the community a better place, as articulated in the policy direction set by the governing board.

Example

City council elections in the City of Sandy occur in November of even-numbered years, and newly-elected council members take office on the following January 1. The council typically holds a full-day Saturday retreat in early February to review its high-level policies and to set goals for the coming biennium and beyond. Department heads are invited to join the council members for the goal-setting discussion. The discussions are informal and collegial, even when individual council members hold widely varying views on the direction of the city and the role of government in meeting community needs.

As a side note, there seems to be a paradox in council-staff relations and policy-setting: the more the staff is willing to relinquish the policy-setting role to the elected officials, the more influence staff has in the development of policy. A colleague once commented, "our city councils have the right to run our cities into the ground, and it is our duty to help them." There is some hyperbole here, but the point is that the members of the city council know when the staff genuinely respects the council's policy leadership role. And when the council members do not feel threatened in that role, they seem to be more willing to listen to staff's input, knowing that they can take it or leave it. Discussions of policies and goals can occur in a civil and thoughtful manner when the discussions are free of power struggles between the council and staff. (There may well be power struggles within the council, and in that case, the staff members are relieved to be able to stand back, out of the fray).

After some wordsmithing, the city council's adopted goals are published on the city web page, and shared with staff in the city manager's payday blog. They eventually reappear in the relevant department's budget narratives, as part of the goals for that department.

The governing body's goals typically focus on projects or major milestones for the government. In a city, they may address planning projects, major capital improvements, or the creation of new services and programs. But what about the day-in and day-out provision of services (e.g., police, library, water, transit, building inspections, etc.) that account for the majority of the city's budget? In this case, once the governing board sets the amount of general tax resources (if any) that will be allocated to the service, the staff's goal is to provide the highest level of service possible with the available resources. An elaborate process in which the governing body specifies outcomes would be a waste of time.

The exception is when there is some kind of shock to the system which requires a major realignment of service levels. In the language of policy theory, the punctuated equilibrium model of policy-setting is a good description of the way budget policy is set by governing bodies.[44]Drawing from Stephen Jay Gould's work in evolutionary biology, punctuated equilibrium in a public policy setting suggests that policy tends to be stable, with only small incremental changes, punctuated by major changes only when the policy system experiences some kind of external shock or push. Both major decreases (as in a recession) and major increases (as in a period of rapid growth) in tax revenues require the governing body to embark on some sort of formal process to set priorities among services. Another trigger for this process would be a major change in the community, whether a natural disaster, or the cumulative effect of demographic changes.

Large and unwieldy governing bodies, such as those of the national and state governments, and some cities and counties, cannot, as a practical matter, arrive at a concise statement of goals for the government. In this case, the policy leadership vacuum is typically filled by an elected politician (president, governor) who serves as the chief executive officer. Here, power struggles over policy-setting are inevitable, and it is more difficult to build trust between members of the legislative body and the staff of the executive branch. But despite the battles highlighted by the media, in most areas there evolves a working consensus on goals and service levels. The line managers responsible for executing the budget typically understand the goals of their organization, even if they are implicitly rather than explicitly supported by the legislative body, when they carry out their

---

[44] Frank Baumgartner and Bryan D. Jones, *Agendas and Instability in American Politics* (Chicago: University of Chicago Press, 1993).

duties of keeping food safe to eat, providing support services for the mentally ill, or operating an interstate highway system.

Setting Budget Targets

A key feature of Theory Y budgeting (and Expenditure Control Budgeting) is the use of budget targets that operating managers are expected to meet, rather than asking departments to submit budget "requests" that are subsequently filtered through the budget process. This is the most challenging aspect of the budget system (at least for the CEO or budget officer) and involves as much art as science.

But for most governments, setting targets isn't as difficult as one would think, because it needs to be done only for those departments or programs that receive support from general taxes (or other general revenues, such as general fund interest earnings). Self-supporting operations (e.g., sewer utilities, building inspections, the US Postal Service) and those with dedicated revenue sources (highway funds, services funded through state lotteries) have built-in targets: expenditures must not exceed revenues (plus beginning balances).

For programs or departments that are at least partially supported by general governmental revenues, the key decision in setting a budget target is that of the amount of the general revenues to be allocated to that area. The department head or operating manager is free to supplement the general revenue with departmental revenues (e.g., grants, user fees) as well as carryover savings.

Many governments use, as a starting point, a formula to set the targets. For example:

The City of Sandy uses the prior year's general revenue amount (with no inflationary increase) and adds any increases to personnel costs for existing staff levels that are set by the city council (e.g., cost of living increase, health and pension increases, other cost increases set by union contracts).

The City of Medford uses last year's target, increased by the *average* of the increase in the consumer price index and the increase in the city's population.

The City of Chandler's target covers non-personnel costs only (on the assumption that COLAs and other personnel cost increases are beyond the direct control of the line departments). It too is incremental, based on the prior year's target. It may be increased by an across-the-board factor reflecting inflation and/or population growth, or in periods of declining revenue, the city manager may apply a deflating factor.

The use of a formula is appealing because it appears to be fair and objective. But it should be a starting point only. If the CEO could prepare a budget for his or her organization by simply relying on a mathematical formula, then the CEO should be replaced by a computer. The fact is, if the CEO or chief financial officer is paying attention, they know which departments have some budget fat and which ones don't. One department head noted: "you know their budget is doing OK when the staff start wearing polo shirts with the department logo embroidered on them."

Example

In Sandy, the targets were tweaked to add dollars when the department was faced with an unusual jump in costs (e.g., a large increase in the amount charged by the county for police dispatch services), or when the operating budget has been squeezed to the point where the manager has run out of options. And the targets can (and should) be adjusted when the governing board changes the priorities for service provision.

Even when formula-based targets are adjusted (and as subjective as those adjustments may seem), department heads tend to readily accept them. The fact that operating managers appear to embrace a fixed target seems surprising given that it usually results in a smaller share of general revenues than when the budget request game is played by a skillful competitor. What accounts for it?

There are probably several parts to the answer. First, most department heads find the usual zero-sum budget games exhausting and demotivating. Even when all departments get an increase in their budgets there is, as with most games, just one winner (the one with the biggest increase) and everyone else (the losers). Second, deep down, most operating managers understand and respect the responsibility of the governing board and CEO to set overall direction for the organization; it is, after all, their job. Setting budget targets is a stronger form of leadership than saying, "show me what you think you need, and I'll let you know if I agree with you." Third, the existence of a target (an admittedly top-down, central management element of the system) is more than offset by the freedom the department heads get in managing the rest of their budget. The message from the CEO is, "I'll make the decision on the share of the general revenue you get, but I trust you to make your own decisions on additional revenues, budget savings, and how you distribute the dollars across your own divisions and line items. And once you make those decisions, I won't pester you about whether you're spending according the plan, but instead trust you to manage your own budget as long as you're producing the outcomes that we've agreed on." For operating managers, the fixed target is a small price to pay for liberation from the usual central budget office tyranny.

Interestingly, at this point, the budget work on the part of the governing body and CEO is essentially finished. The process from now on (at least from their perspective) is anticlimactic. The governing body has provided its policy direction in the form of goals and program priorities, and it expect the staff to carry them out. The CEO, armed with long range forecasts of general revenues, knows that the budget will balance with the targets that have been given to the departments. The CEO (and governing board) will be curious about how much service, or how many projects, will be able to be provided with the available resources, but the difficult budget decisions by the government's top leadership have already been made. There may be some remaining minor decisions on the fringes of the budget. A manager may need to make a decision that has budget implications—for example, between the size of the book collection and the open hours of the library system—where policy guidance would be helpful. But these kinds of decisions will be rare and relatively insignificant.

A potential pitfall is that the governing body and CEO will see their counterparts in other organizations (with the usual Theory X budget systems) going through a knock-down drag-out process of making painful budget decisions, and begin to worry that they're not doing their jobs. The CEO or CFO might be tempted to manufacture something that looks like the typical budget hearing process by setting the department targets low enough to leave a small pile of money for the governing body to play with. This temptation should be avoided, for two reasons. First, it is actually insulting to the governing body, since it sends the message "we as staff will take care of the 98% of the budget we really care about, and leave you to wrestle over the other two percent." Of course, this is exactly what happens in most incremental Theory X budget systems (even in supposedly zero-based systems, budget decisions come down to relatively small increases or decreases to the previous year's base). The Theory Y process emphasizes that the governing body sets the goals and direction for *the entire budget*, and once it has done that, steps back to leave staff to the task of figuring how to meet the goals it with available resources (and then to hold the staff accountable for the outcomes).

Second, even a mini budget game is still a budget game, and many of the benefits of a Theory Y process are lost if the governing body and staff are made to play it. In a year of unusually high population growth (with corresponding growth in the tax base) the author forgot this advice, and asked the management team to come up with suggestions on how to allocate revenues that well exceeded the departments' combined targets. The silence in the conference room was deafening: the department heads refused to even start the game. And there was no excuse for it. The city council had been clear on what its priorities were, including a healthy wish-list of programs and services it would like to provide given sufficient resources (e.g., a higher level of street preventive maintenance). The city manager's job was to act in accordance with that direction, and adjust (increase) targets as necessary to reflect the council's priorities in light of a spurt in revenue growth.

Lengthening the Budget Period

A Theory Y budget process makes it relatively easy to jettison the typical annual budget cycle, and set budgets in longer increments (at least 24 months, if not longer—see Chapter 5). The choice of a budget period may seem to be a separate issue from the management philosophy that underlies the budget process, but in fact the two issues are closely linked.

A city manager colleague once commented that he wasn't in favor of a two-year budget process, since a city's financial circumstances can change so quickly that even an annual process can't keep up with changes in the economy. This comment belies a Theory X philosophy: it assumes the central administrator is the only one to pilot the organization through a financial storm. But a Theory Y approach decentralizes budget decision-making, and along with it, the information and resources needed to respond to changes in the external environment. The recreation manager is in a much better position than the finance director (or central accountant or budget analyst) to both notice a drop-off in team registrations and to make necessary program adjustments. The building official sees directly an increase in inspection response times during a surge in building activity; he or she is in the best position to use the accompanying surge in permit fees to hire part-time or contract inspectors. By the same token, the building official is in the best position to hold off on filling a vacant inspector position when he or she has noticed that the volume of plan checks (a leading indicator of building permit applications) has dropped.

One could argue that only the central administration is in a position to monitor and respond to changes in general revenues, such as sales tax or income tax, and should therefore control all departmental expenditures. Not true, for two reasons.

First, most responsible governments establish a fund reserve to act as a spring to absorb short-term increases or decreases in volatile revenue sources. They also use conservative estimates for these sources to avoid the need for panic-driven mid-course budget cuts.

Second, once targets are set, general revenues can be directly allocated to departments, prorated according to the original target amounts. In this way, the departments themselves can react to both increases and decreases in actual revenues compared to the initial estimates. As long as the operating managers are accountable for the bottom line, the organization now has built-in mechanisms to adjust to changing economic conditions, without the need for intervention by the central administration.

This does put a greater burden on the operating managers, since external conditions are by definition beyond their direct control (all they can control is their spending in

SCOTT DOUGLAS LAZENBY

response to changes in general revenues). But for them, it is a small price to pay to be free of the headaches of an annual cycle. Note that for many governments, the budget preparation process is so long that most managers begin working on a new budget even before the next one is adopted, at the same time they are managing a current budget and working on the audit for last year's budget.

A 24-month budget period cuts the number-crunching burden in half. It frees up time for the governing body to devote to other things; for example, a thorough (and qualitative) review of programs and performance measures; setting a long term capital improvement plan; reviewing forecasts and rate models for utilities, etc. It encourages the governing body and staff to take a longer-term view of their policies; for example, the operating cost of a new facility is more likely to show up in the operating budget if the budget period is longer than twelve months.

And in the rare occasions when changes in external conditions are so precipitous that it is beyond the capacity of the operating manager(s) to respond, there is always a process for budget amendments. Even here, mid-course changes usually affect only a portion of the government's programs and services.

Example

In Sandy, a biennial budget cycle meshes very well with city council elections and goal-setting:

1. November of even-numbered years—election of mayor and three council members (on four-year staggered terms).

THE HUMAN SIDE OF BUDGETING

2. January, odd numbered years—new council members take office.
3. February—council goal-setting retreat.
4. March-June—preparation of the budget for the next biennium. This gives newly-elected council members enough time to become familiar with their roles and city issues, but also allows them to influence a new budget fairly early in their term.
5. July 1—new budget in effect (for 24 months).

The Mechanics of the Process: The Line Department's View

Up to this point, the elements of a Theory Y budget process are fairly easy to grasp. Many agencies already use a process for developing organizational goals. Some use target-based budgets.

It is when the line agency managers assemble their budgets that things begin to look very different. General fund departments that never had to deal with revenues suddenly find themselves focusing on their net budget, not total expenditures. Year-end (or biennium-end) estimates suddenly become more important, because they are used to calculate carryover savings. Balancing to a bottom line target adds another level of complexity, and also new opportunities for creativity. Departmental contingency accounts eliminate the need to pad line items, so line item estimates become "best guess" rather than "worst case" projections.

This section will step through the mechanics of budget preparation under a Theory Y process. Examples, based on a simplified budget for a police department's budget, will help visualize the concepts. Note that the examples are just that. There may well be better ways to design the mechanics of a Theory Y process.

A Bottom-Line Approach

All departments, even general fund internal functions such as accounting, can produce revenue, and can use this revenue to offset expenditures. If nothing else, departments generate carryover savings, which appear in the budget as a revenue source (beginning balance). The focus of departments shifts from total expenditures to the bottom line, including revenues. In a Theory X process, it is the central finance function that carries the burden of monitoring the bottom line (i.e., are *both* revenues and expenditures matching the budget estimates?). Under a Theory Y process, this responsibility is decentralized to the operating departments.

In a self-balancing fund, such as a "proprietary" (or "enterprise") fund used to account for a utility (e.g., a water system, or the Bonneville Power Administration), the bottom line is simply revenues less expenditures, just as it is for a business. Expenses may be coming in higher than estimated, but if revenues are coming in even stronger, the bottom line is healthy: the fund is operating in the black. If expenses exceed revenues, the bottom line is a negative number, signifying the fund is operating at a loss. This may be planned (as in the case of a healthy balance that has been accumulated for the specific purpose of upgrading infrastructure), but the negative (red) number is a signal that the pattern is not sustainable in the long term.

General fund departments—partially or fully funded through general revenues—are a different matter. When expenditures are subtracted from departmental revenues, the resulting bottom line is almost always negative. This poses a few problems. First, in this case, the negative number is not necessarily bad. It signifies that the department receives general revenues to supplement its own revenues. Second, most mortals have a hard time working with negative numbers. Suppose the *budgeted* bottom line is $-250,000 and the *actual* bottom line is $-275,000. Is this a bad thing or a good thing? (It's bad, but this isn't immediately apparent.) And how do you calculate budget savings? Normally, you calculate budget savings by subtracting the actual expenses from the budgeted expenses. But here—using the negative bottom line numbers—this calculation would yield a *positive* $25,000, which looks like savings even though the financial performance was *worse* than budgeted.

The solution is simple. In addition to allocating direct departmental revenues to each department, treat all general fund departments as mini enterprise (self-balancing) funds, and show general revenue support as simply another source of revenue for the department. Therefore, *budgeted* (i.e., estimated) revenues always equal budgeted expenditures. The bottom line (total revenues less expenditures) for the budget would be zero. The bottom line for *actual* financial results would be positive (a good thing) when revenues are coming in better than estimated or expenditures are coming in lower than estimated (or both), and negative (bad) when the opposite occurs.

This approach does require more work by the central accounting staff. They still need to track overall tax receipts, and will want a single revenue line item (accounted for in a general revenue "department") to account for each major tax source. But they can create a separate "distribution to departments" expense line item that is debited periodically (monthly or quarterly) as the tax revenue is credited to the various departments. This does create some double counting when the "total budget" for the organization is calculated, but due to the perverseness of fund accounting, governmental budgets are replete with double counting, and everyone except the press understands that the "total budget" is a meaningless number.

The example below gives a highly simplified picture of two general fund departments: one used to account for general revenues, and the police department. The amount of general revenue allocated to the police department is highlighted as an expenditure of the "general revenues" department and a revenue of the police department. In preparing the budget, the police chief can't change (increase) this number, but he or she can change other revenues and operating expenses, as long as total departmental revenues and expenditures continue to equal each other.

	Revenue	Expenditures
General Revenues Dept		
Nondept Beginning Balance	$1,000,000	
Taxes, franchises, etc.	$3,000,000	
Distribution to Depts		
Library		$200,000
Police		**$2,600,000**
Parks		$200,000
Other		$1,000,000
Total, General Revenues	**$4,000,000**	**$4,000,000**
Police		
Beginning Balance	$50,000	
Departmental Revenues	$300,000	
General Revenues	**$2,600,000**	
Operating Expenses		$2,800,000
Overhead Costs		$150,000
Total, Police	**$2,950,000**	**$2,950,000**

Calculating Year-End Estimates

Even though line item budgets are a very poor way to convey financial information for policy discussions (they force the focus on the means, rather than the ends, of public services), they are the workhorse of budget estimating and tracking by managers. Under a Theory Y system, the process of developing year-end estimates is similar to that of a Theory X system, but interestingly, the resulting estimates will probably be different. Specifically, estimates for spending will probably be *lower* (and more accurate) under a Theory Y system than under the traditional Theory X system. Why?

The answer is in the rules of the game. Under a Theory X process, year-end estimates are produced for two reasons: first, to give the central budgeting staff a way to estimate the government's total year-end spending (by aggregating the department's estimates); and second, to provide background information upon which to judge the department's request for the next year's budget. It is the latter use of year-end estimates that creates a strong incentive to inflate the numbers. The manager knows the central budget analyst will rely heavily on actual spending trends as an indicator of the appropriate budget amounts for each line item. Therefore, to produce evidence that a large budget is justified, the manager will need to ensure that both actual spending *and* the estimates for year-end expenditures are as high as possible (yet still within the appropriation limit).

Under a Theory Y process, the only purpose of year-end estimates is for the operating manager to calculate year-end savings (and thus carryover amounts), and to build a line item budget for the next period. So in this case, there is no incentive to pad the estimates. Departments do tend to be conservative, since *underestimating* year-end spending means less carryover than budgeted. On the other hand, overestimating year-end spending may result in a pleasant surprise when the financial dust settles at the end of the year, but if the difference is large, the manager may have to jump through some extra hoops to actually spend the difference, depending on the amount of budgetary freedom that is actually granted to the manager (more on this later).

The amount of the carryover (beginning balance for the next year) is made up of both expenditure savings *and* revenues that exceed estimates.

POLICE	Estimated	Actual (Year-End Estimate)
Revenues		
Beginning Balance	$50,000	$75,000
Dept. Revenues	$300,000	$295,000
General Revenues	$2,600,000	$2,600,000
TOTAL REVENUES	**$2,950,000**	**$2,970,000**
Expenses		
Operating Expenses	$2,800,000	$2,750,000
Overhead Costs	$1500,00	$150,000
TOTAL EXPENSES	**$2,950,000**	**$2,90,000**

In this case, the carryover amount is $70,000. If budgeted expenditures equal budgeted revenues for all general fund programs, this is simply the estimated revenue ($2,970,000) less the estimated actual expenditure ($2,900,000) for the program. Or, it can be calculated as actual revenue less budgeted revenue ($2,970,000 - $2,950,000) plus budgeted expenditures less actual expenditures ($2,950,000 - $2,900,000); the result is the same.

What if the manager projects that he or she will *overspend* the budget? In that case, the carryover amount is a negative number, and the budgeted beginning balance for the program or department is also negative. In other words, the responsibility falls on the operating manager to dig himself or herself out of the budgetary hole in the next fiscal year (or biennium).

If this happens habitually for a department, it signifies a management problem, not a problem with the budget system. But unlike the traditional budget system, it holds the manager accountable for budgetary performance. In a Theory X system, the overspending manager may receive some kind of discipline (often nothing more than passing mention in an annual performance review), but it is up to the central budgeting staff to deal with the overage (typically by offsetting it with savings gained by other departments, or through agency-wide contingency accounts). Under a Theory Y process, the line manager must deal with it.

If the overage is large, it could cause cash flow problems for the government. But in a well-managed organization, it shouldn't be a surprise to anyone. With proper financial reporting, the operating manager should be the first to know of the problem, and if he or she has run out of options to address it, will bring the problem to the attention of the CEO. This is an admission of defeat, and seems to be a rare occurrence in ECB systems.

Building a Budget Based on a Target

As noted above, setting budget targets for programs and departments is a much an art as a science. It is the most challenging aspect of the process for the CEO, since it requires both a clear view of the governing board's priorities, and intimate knowledge of the resources and constraints available to the operating managers in managing their budgets.

But for the operating managers, the target is simply a given. Their challenge lies in building a budget that is realistic but still meets the target. It is typically an iterative process: the manager builds a detailed line item budget (covering both revenues and expenditures), relying on data on past trends as well as knowledge of future challenges, and checks the bottom line against the target. If the bottom line is less than the target, the manager has the happy task of adding expenditures (service increases, equipment or facilities, etc.). If it exceeds the target (probably more typical), the manager faces the challenge of either finding additional sources of revenue, reducing planned expenditures, or both.

In the example below, the amount of general revenues allocated to the police department (highlighted) is a fixed quantity (the target). Other amounts can be varied by the police chief, as long as total expenditures match total revenues.

	Budget (next biennium)	Notes
Police – Revenues		
Beginning Balance	$70,000	1
Traffic Fines	$300,000	
Fingerprinting	$25,000	2

Reports	$30,000	2
Grants	$150,000	
Misc	$40,000	
General Revenues	**$2,600,000**	3
Total, Police Revenues	**$3,215,000**	
Police - Expenditures		
Salary & Benefits	$2,145,000	4
Vehicle expenses	$300,000	
Operating supplies	200,000	
Equipment, including patrol cars	350,000	
Contingency	$70,000	
Overhead Costs	$150,000	5
Total, Police Expenditures	**$3,215,000**	

Notes

1 Based on carryover calculation

2 Department sets rates but doesn't control demand

3 This amount cannot be changed by the department; it is the key element of the department's budget target

4 Pay classifications and benefit costs may be beyond the control of the department, but the department does control the number and level of positions

5 Department may not have much control over this cost in the short term, but can influence long term costs

Contingency Accounts

All resourceful budget managers keep their own contingency accounts, to give them some flexibility to respond to unforeseen circumstances. In Theory X systems, these accounts take the form of line item padding, where budgets for certain line items are set larger than truly necessary. These line items are typically obscure, or for types of expenditures that experience wide swings (credit card merchant fees, miscellaneous expenses, licensing fees, etc.). They do not include line items that often receive extra scrutiny, such as travel and training. In fact, these line items are often under budgeted, knowing that savings in the padded line items can be used as justification for over spending.

A Theory Y system makes these contingency accounts explicit, and departments are encouraged to establish them. This is good management: contingencies *do* arise, and managers should have resources at their disposal to deal with them. The carryover savings program gives them an incentive not to use the contingency account unless they have to, but it's there if they need it. And a side benefit is that, with no need to pad line items, the budgeted amounts for line items are more useful for operating managers because they more accurately reflect their estimate of actual costs.

Example
During a decade of record housing construction, Sandy's planning and development department built up a large contingency account, exceeding the annual operating cost of the department. The City Council was well aware of it, but resisted the temptation to

spend it down (in other areas), knowing that the construction industry was highly cyclical. When the downturn did hit, it hit hard, and development fees nearly disappeared. The department had a very small staff, so dialing down positions would have been difficult. Instead, the contingency account served as a buffer: the department was able to meet payroll until housing construction picked up again. The planners turned their attention to much-needed housekeeping changes to the development code, and the building official managed small remodel projects in city facilities.

As a technical note, expenditures should not be made directly from a contingency account. This obscures the actual use of the money. Instead, as the fiscal year progresses, the *budget* for the contingency account can be reduced, and the budget for other line items increased. Or the manager can simply overspend line items, knowing that the contingency serves as a buffer when managing the bottom line.

Budget Review

This process does not require that the CEO and governing board abrogate their responsibility for stewardship of public resources and overall leadership of the organization. It is entirely appropriate for them to review the decisions the operating managers make in developing their budgets. When difficult decisions are involved, the managers may actually seek the support and concurrence of the organization's leaders.

But this review should be of the "trust and verify" variety. Knowing that departments have built-in incentives to be efficient, the governing body should avoid the usual pecking around in line items and debating the appropriate amount to spend on paper clips. The governing board should be cautious in modifying the target amounts set by the CEO: if the operating managers get the idea that the targets are soft and can be adjusted upward by a persuasive argument to the governing board, then much of the benefit of target-based budgeting is lost. In an emergency, the governing body can always raid the contingency accounts within the departments, or temporarily suspend the carryover program. In a true emergency, the managers understand and accept it. But if it is done capriciously, the managers will simply adapt to the new rules of the game, to the long term peril of the organization.

Above all, the review should focus on outcomes, not inputs. This concept isn't new: it is a recurring theme in much of the recent literature on reform of budget processes. But in many cases, an outcome-based budget decision-making process rides on top of an unreformed Theory X budget management philosophy, with the traditional game-playing in budget requests, padded line items, and year-end spending "shenanigans."

The policy makers can be more comfortable in focusing on goals and outcomes (as they should) if they are confident that the rules of budget management have been changed so that the operating managers are encouraged to be efficient, innovative, and careful stewards of the government's resources.

Budget Management

State law requires many local governments to adhere to the traditional (expenditure) appropriation process: the adopted budget will have to specify legal limits on total spending by each department or program. But a Theory Y process should allow managers to ignore these limits.

Consider the following example. A school district operated an indoor swimming pool at a loss. The pool manager found that she could reduce the net drain on the general fund through sales of swim goggles. But after only a quarter of the fiscal year, she had reached her appropriation limit for supplies. Even though increased expenditures would have been more than matched by increased revenue, she was prohibited from purchasing more goggles to sell.

Under a Theory Y budget process, the pool manager would be encouraged to spend more in order to earn more. The manager would still be responsible for the bottom line, but in the system outlined here, this means that expenditures will not exceed revenues (including the agreed-upon allocation of general revenue).

In practice this requires, near the end of the fiscal year or biennium, a series of budget amendments that are housekeeping items only. Where possible, they can simply be placed on a consent agenda, with no further discussion (in Sandy, it was informally referred to as "the cleanup resolution").

Of far more substantive importance is vigilance on the part of operating managers to ensure that the bottom line results are healthy (revenues meet or exceed expenditures). They need detailed and quick reports on the financial performance of their operations. Compared to a century ago, modern technology actually makes this feasible (the heavy centralization of the "administrative science" era could have been justified purely on the basis of the practical difficulty in producing financial reports). Modern general ledger systems can provide on-line real-time revenue and expenditure details to operating managers, or for that matter, anyone in the world (Sandy uses a web database interface to make real-time financial data available to the public as well as city departments).

Departments should have full freedom to shift resources across line items, and department heads should have freedom to move resources across various programs they oversee. They can either do this by shifting budget amounts (e.g., increasing one line item's budget and decreasing another by the same amount), or by simply (and consciously) over spending one line item and under spending another. The choice should be theirs. The former is helpful in managing the budget, especially if relatively large dollar amounts are involved. But there is nothing wrong with the latter approach: it is the bottom line result that matters.

Internal Budget Management Policies

Delegating more budget decision-making authority to operating managers requires them to carry more of the burden of responsibility for the organization's financial health, and for adherence to sound financial management practices. The departments should not be micro-managed, but it is appropriate for the governing body and CEO to place appropriate limits on their authority.

For example, a financially-prudent policy is to **use one-time revenues for one-time expenses only**. There are obvious risks in using one-time revenue to hire new staff (with a continuing obligation to cover salary and benefit expenses), or to pay for recurring costs such as building utilities. Therefore, governments using Expenditure Control Budgeting often restrict the use of carryover funds (beginning balances) to one-time expenditures only, such as for equipment or capital improvements, or increases in the department's contingency account.

Departments may also be given limits on dollar amounts for purchases of equipment or capital facilities, or for new service contracts, that can be included in the budget without formal review and approval by the governing body. These limits should be set as high as possible, and the governing body members should be cautious in second-guessing their professional staff. As noted above, the review should be consistent with a "trust and verify" philosophy, but it is appropriate since the governing body is ultimately accountable for the activities of the government.

The governing body may also need to formally approve certain types of new revenue: grants over a given dollar amount, some classes of user fees, and so on.

Conclusion

There are procedural changes in moving to a Theory Y budget system; number-crunching looks different. But to focus on these elements would be to miss the management philosophy that serves as the foundation for the process. The Theory Y budget system **supports and complements** an organizational culture of trust and openness, where operating managers and their staff are treated as thinking people who truly want to make the world a better place. It helps fulfill a philosophy of decentralization and empowerment that is only given lip service in so many organizations. It allows good managers to actually practice what they preach.

Critical elements include:

- Tight alignment between citizen needs and priorities, governing body policies and goals, and budget decisions made by operating managers.

- Decentralizing budget management, so the organization can better respond to changes in the financial climate, and in turn, the budget period can be lengthened.

- Allocating general revenues (targets) to general fund departments based on service priorities, forecasts of available general revenues, and a good understanding of the financial condition of each program or department.

- Allocating all other revenues directly to general fund departments.

- Allowing managers to carry over savings (including the difference between estimated and actual departmental revenue).

- Giving managers the ability to increase a program's total budget by being creative and resourceful in securing additional sources of program revenue.

- Encouraging the creation of departmental contingency accounts.

- Eliminating the budget "request" process.

- Managing to the bottom line, allowing departments to shift resources across line items and programs, and giving them latitude to exceed appropriations when spending is matched by revenue increases.

7

THEORY Y BUDGETING:
IMPLEMENTATION AND OPTIONS

In theory there is no difference between theory and practice. In practice there is.

—Yogi Berra

Even if one fully buys into the philosophy behind Theory Y budgeting, attempting it in practice inevitably raises a number of questions. Should operating managers really be allowed to carry forward *all* their savings? Many Americans (including a lot of us who should know better) do an appalling job managing their personal finances; do we really want to let them manage public finances? If we *require* department heads to adhere to the same philosophy in delegating budget authority to their own program managers, aren't we falling into the dictatorial, micro-managing behavior of Theory X?

This chapter explores many of these issues. Organizations (mostly cities) have had enough experience with these concepts to provide some answers to the practical questions. But the field of social psychology still has much to learn, and much to contribute to this topic. It can be a rich area for research as well as reflective practice.

Do We Carry Over 100% of Savings, or Something Less?

Some early experimenters with Expenditure Control Budgeting allowed operating managers to carry over some, but not all, of their budget savings (e.g., 50%).[45] There are two reasons for this. First, there is a natural tendency for the CEO and governing board to want to have access to some unallocated beginning balance for equipment, capital improvements, or pet projects. If the general fund's beginning balance is scattered across a multitude of program and departmental budgets, it would not be available for large one-time projects or investments.

Second, it's hard to argue that all of the savings are due to the hard work and excellent management of the manager and his or her staff. Surely some percentage of it is due to luck, revenue windfalls, delays in hiring caused by the HR department, good deals in materials and contracts negotiated by the purchasing department, an overly-generous target budget, etc. Why reward operating managers for something they didn't do?

These arguments belie a Theory X philosophy, and we'll return to them in a moment. But aside from the issue of management philosophy, there is a strong pragmatic reason

---

[45] Eric B. Herzik, "Improving Budgetary Management and Fostering Innovation: Expenditure Control Budgeting," *Public Productivity & Management Review,* 14 No. 3, 1991, 237-248.

for allowing operating managers to carry forward *all* of their savings: anything less seriously weakens the disincentive for playing the "spend it or lose it" game. Operating managers aren't idiots. When faced with a choice between losing half their savings, or being able to keep as much of it as possible through a year-end spending spree, they will choose the latter. Creating a discipline of saving for the future is hard enough, since we as humans naturally discount the value of future spending compared to current spending. To further discount the value of future resources through an arbitrary "tax" on the savings seriously undermines this discipline.

Returning to the arguments for splitting the savings, note that in a Theory Y culture, individuals act as good managers (and stewards of public resources) not because they are bribed or otherwise rewarded for doing so, but because of the *intrinsic* reward of doing good work. Allowing managers to carry over savings is not some kind of reward; it is simply a way to give them more flexibility in the use of resources to get the job done. The accounting system's annual (or biannual) budget clock is completely arbitrary, and has nothing to do with the continuing demand on resources faced by managers as they provide services to the public. We wouldn't expect the revenues of an enterprise fund (e.g., a sewer utility, or the Tennessee Valley Authority) to magically and arbitrarily disappear when the accountants' fiscal year begins. The same should hold for programs within the general fund; whether savings are due to management skill or dumb luck, they should be available to the manager to help him or her meet continuing service challenges and unanticipated contingencies.

A CEO can choose to "keep" some of the departments'

carryover savings, but in this case, the program is just a variant of the traditional Theory X budget system, in which the CEO (and other central staff functions) are presumed to be better and smarter at allocating the organization's resources. A rule that allows only partial carryover of savings sends a perverse mixed message on trust: "I trust you to manage your resources...but only so far." It's insulting, like throwing a bone to a dog.

For those who truly want their organization's systems to align with a culture of trust, openness, and empowerment, there is no choice but to allow managers to keep all their savings. But this still leaves the practical problem of finding resources to fund priorities of the governing board that don't fall neatly into one of the operating programs, or exceed the resources available to any single program.

Fortunately, there are several solutions that don't involve poisoning the health of a carryover savings program:

- Most governments have some form of general governmental expenses that are budgeted for in one or more "non-departmental" accounts. They may include city hall utility expenses, general liability premiums, contracted legal and audit services, dues for organization-wide memberships, etc. Good budget practice would minimize the use of these kinds of accounts, since responsibility for managing expenses is diffused across multiple individuals (or entities) within the organization. But savings in this budget can be a source of the mad money that governing boards like to spend on projects.

- Similarly, the general fund includes, by definition, general tax revenue that is not legally dedicated to a specific program or service. Revenues that are generated above the estimated amount can either be allocated to departments in proportion to their budgeted allotment of general taxes *or* retained centrally to give the CEO and governing board some added flexibility.

- A year-end bounty of general revenue "surplus" can be almost guaranteed if tax revenues are intentionally underestimated. But in the spirit of openness and anti-game-playing, it is better to estimate revenues as accurately as possible, and simply set aside some of it in the budget (for future allocation) before setting the departmental target budgets.

- In many cases, the organization needs to carve out resources that will ultimately benefit (or be used by) multiple departments. Suppose, for example, a county wants to fund a major expansion of its field operations center on a pay-as-you-go basis, rather than trying to get voters to authorize bonds for it. The using departments could be charged (e.g., as a premium on their normal internal "rent" payments) over time to build up a pool of cash that would then fund the improvement.

- In some cases, departmental carryover amounts can accumulate to fairly large levels. As long as the operating manager is allowed to keep a reasonable contingency account and as long as it is done with care and good judgment, the CEO and governing body can tap into this accumulation without seriously undermining the benefits of Theory Y budgeting.

- In a true emergency, operating managers understand that the governing board has not only a right, but a duty, to use any resources necessary (including departmental contingency accounts) to respond to the emergency. But this only applies if the emergency is generally acknowledged as such; it would not include bailing out the fire department to offset the cost of a lavish union contract.

In a healthy organization, there should be minimal need for the governing body or CEO to have a source of their "own" money: when the priorities of the governing board and the operating managers are aligned (as they should be in a representative democracy), the operating managers will act to carry out the wishes and desires of the governing board.

What About Gainsharing?

Some governments have advocated "gainsharing," where staff are paid bonuses for saving money. Would this be a better, or more powerful, incentive to offset the advantages of a year-end spending spree?

There are many arguments against doing this. First, a number of studies have found that *intrinsic* motivation (an internal drive to do something) is more powerful than *extrinsic* motivation (an external reward for behavior).[46] Getting paid more to spend less than the budgeted amount is an extrinsic motivator. Operating more efficiently in order to carry over savings and thus have more resource flexibility in the future

---

[46] See, for example, Daniel Pink, *Drive: The Surprising Truth About What Motivates Us* (Riverhead, 2011).

THE HUMAN SIDE OF BUDGETING

taps into the intrinsic motivation of the desire to be a good manager.

Second, an operating manager can achieve savings (and thus guarantee a bonus) in several ways: certainly by operating more efficiently, but also by withholding service to the public or by padding the budget. There are enough perverse incentives in most public agencies that it makes little sense to create a new one in which taxpayers pay government employees a financial reward to provide less public service.

Third and most important, gainshairing and other pay-for-performance systems treat employees like prostitutes, sending the message that they need to be bribed to rise above mediocre performance.

Should Department Heads be Required to Use Theory Y Budgeting with their Program Managers?

All managers, regardless of how they view their own employees, seem to like being on the receiving end of Theory Y budgeting: they all appreciate the increased flexibility and autonomy the process provides. For small organizations with few mid managers, it may not matter much (at least from a budgeting standpoint) whether the department heads really buy into a Theory Y philosophy of management, since when preparing budgets, the buck stops there.

But larger organizations have several layers of managers who have authority over spending as well as revenues such as user fees and grants. A Theory X department head may be confident of his or her own ability to manage a budget, but take a dim view of the abilities of subordinates, and impose a Theory X system on them. Specifically, the department head might directly (or indirectly with departmental budget analysts) prepare the budgets for subordinate divisions or program managers, or at best put them through a competitive request process for a share of the department's budget target. He or she might control all requisitions and spending in order to reserve the ability to make all decisions on allocating carryover savings.

If the CEO *requires* department heads to use a Theory Y process within their own departments, a department head might respond, "You talk about empowerment and giving us the authority to manage our own operations, and now you're dictating the way we handle our own budget process within the department. That's not empowerment, that's micromanaging."

Or is it? Peters and Waterman, in *In Search of Excellence,* emphasize the "loose-tight" principle.[47] The CEO and organization should be inflexible ("tight") on the core values and culture that define the organization; for example, excellent customer service, an obsession for high quality work, ethics and integrity, etc. They should be flexible ("loose") on the steps employees take to achieve the goals of the organization, as long as the core values are maintained.

A Theory Y philosophy, which treats employees as thinking human beings who want to do a good job, must be one of the core values that allows for no exceptions within the organization; it must be a foundational element of the organization's culture. Especially in a transitional period, not all department heads or mid managers will really believe in it; some will, in their heart, subscribe to a Theory X belief that

---

[47]Thomas Peters & Robert Waterman, *In Search of Excellence* (HarperCollins, 1982).

their employees are lazy and stupid. They must, however, be required to act and manage as if they truly subscribed to the (new) philosophy. Over time, some of these Theory X managers will in fact change their view of people (they will be pleasantly surprised). Others will be replaced over time; the new managers who are hired or promoted should be selected on the basis of their adherence to the organization's values.

The same process modeled by the CEO should be followed at every level of management within the organization:

- Department heads with several general fund programs should give each program manager a budget target, and give the program managers maximum flexibility in developing and managing a budget within the target.

- To the maximum extent possible, control over spending should be decentralized, wherever the program manager has influence over the cost of providing public services. This certainly includes operating supplies and personnel costs associated with different staffing levels, but might also include office space leases, contract costs for internal or external IT and HR services, and vehicle fleet costs. The same holds true for revenues.

- Program managers should be allowed to carry over their own program savings.

Which Department Gets Traffic Fine Revenue?

In a typical city, several programs or divisions work

together in a process that ultimately results in someone paying a traffic fine: officers in the police department's patrol division write the ticket, a clerk in the police department's records unit may transcribe it into a computerized system, and the municipal court adjudicates the citation. Depending on the seriousness of the offense, the city attorney might get involved. So an obvious question in a Theory Y system is: which program gets the revenue?

It is possible to split the revenue; for example, to allocate half of it to the police department and half to the municipal court. But there are some disadvantages to doing so. Some automated accounting systems can code revenues to multiple accounts on a fixed percentage basis, but most can't. So allocating the a fine payment to multiple revenue accounts could involve some time-consuming manual effort.

A more serious issue is replacing one set of bad rules (i.e., allowing department heads to leave revenue responsibility to a central finance function) for another set of bad rules. Drivers often believe that speed traps are set up to allow the police departments (or officer) to meet a quota for number of tickets issued or traffic fines generated. Since fine revenue typically accounts for a small fraction of the cost of operating a police department, this belief is probably more urban myth than reality. And officers often find traffic work unpleasant—ticketed drivers are unhappy at best and a serious safety threat at worst—and some incentive to do it could help support the governing body's goal of improved traffic safety.

Traffic fine revenue is typically a large fraction of the cost of operating a municipal court. Judges (and court clerks with authority delegated by the judge) have discretion over fine amounts, and their objectivity might be questioned if there was strong budgetary pressure to keep fine levels high. On the other hand, if there is *no* budgetary consequence of reducing fines, the judges and clerks might be biased in favor of doing so, since there is no apparent consequence in being overly lenient.

The lesson here—and it can be generalized to other areas in which multiple departments or programs have a key role in generating a single source of revenue—is the answer can only come from careful thought, and a good understanding of the cause-and-effect relationship between management of the program and the level of revenue generated, as well as an appreciation of the governing board's priorities.

"My Money"

During an informal budget discussion, city council members sat around a table with the planning director and talked about new initiatives they were interested in. One was a tree planting program that would increase the number of street trees and park foliage. The council members noticed the planning department had a very healthy contingency account, and wondered if that could be used for the new "urban forestry" program. The planning director, who had a green thumb herself, said, "that would be an appropriate use of my money." The city manager almost kicked her under the table.

It was not, of course, *her* money; it was the taxpayers' money, and the members of the city council were elected to be the stewards of that money. At least at an intellectual level, the planning director fully understood that fact and would have obeyed whatever budget decision the council made.

Nonetheless, under a Theory Y budget system, operating managers are given both the responsibility and the resources to do their jobs. The CEO *wants* them to treat the taxpayers' money as if it were their own. It's also healthy for department heads to have a personal compassion for their department's mission. So the potential always exists for a test of will over who gets to make the ultimate decisions on the use of the taxpayers' money.

The solution is *not* to beat the operating managers into submission, and make them become indifferent administrators of budgets they don't care about. A better approach is to constantly remind the operating managers that their job is to fulfill the needs and priorities of the citizens *as defined by the governing body*, and to look for opportunities to celebrate the good work of staff that, as a result of their resourcefulness and management skill, helps the members of the governing board achieve their goals for the organization.

What About Programs that Don't Generate Revenue?

A Theory Y approach encourages operating managers to pay attention to the bottom line, and to look for both efficiency in operating costs as well as ways to preserve or increase revenues. But some programs or units really don't generate much in the way of non-tax revenue. These include highway maintenance departments (in the absence of toll roads), park maintenance (where park use is free), most public libraries, and many social service units. And internal staff functions—human resources, legal services, finance—

typically don't generate external user fees or grants.

In these situations, most of the benefits of a Theory Y budget system still apply: target-based budgeting, carryover savings, flexibility over line items. And the *possibility* of finding new revenue sources (that are acceptable to the governing body) can bring to the surface new ideas that may not have occurred to the finance department in a Theory X system.

And why not establish internal user fees for staff functions? Gifford and Elizabeth Pinchot, in *The End of Bureaucracy,* argue that organizations can keep overhead costs under control by giving line departments discretion over whether to use in-house staff services, or to contract with outside providers.[48] Barzelay reports that the State of Minnesota experimented with splitting staff regulatory functions from support functions, and putting the latter on a fully discretionary, optional basis (even encouraging different departments to compete for internal "customers").[49] For example, a small group with representatives from multiple departments was assigned the regulatory function of setting standards for IT systems and inter-department compatibility; IT support service was split off into a separate unit where it had to compete with outside contractors for the line departments' business.

Spending staff time to establish internal prices and to set up and manage the requisite cost accounting system does add to overhead costs and thus reduces efficiency. But many have argued that this cost is small compared to the advantages to

---

[48] Gifford & Elizabeth Pinchot, *End of Bureaucracy and the Rise of the Intelligent Organization* (Berrett-Koehler, 1993).

[49] Michael Barzelay, *Breaking Through Bureaucracy: A New Vision for Managing in Government* (University of California Press, 1992).

the organization in countering the natural bloat (in staff and budgets) of internal staff functions, and the tendency (especially in larger bureaucracies) for internal staff units to begin to dominate the line departments that are doing the actual work of the organization.

A Theory Y budgeting system lends itself especially well to a management philosophy that acknowledges that internal staff functions exist solely to support the work of the line departments. If they are to be accountable to their internal "customers," they also need flexibility over line items and the ability to carry over savings. And those that can be fully self-supporting (on internal user fees) should set their own budgets.

What About Large Bureaucracies that Perform Routine Services?

Consider a typical state Department of Motor Vehicles (DMV) office. Most of the administrative decisions for the office are made centrally: land and office space leases, development of software and maintenance of the computer system, purchase of standard forms and driver manuals, negotiation of union contracts and establishment of salary scales, and even hiring. Prices (license fees) are set centrally, often by the legislature. The local office manager acts as the day-to-day supervisor of the office staff, and may participate in hiring decisions, but otherwise has little influence over operating costs or revenues. These individuals need not have much training or skill in financial management, or even efficiency improvement. Is there any reason to use a Theory Y budget process in this situation?

There is no point in giving individuals responsibility for a budget when the organization prevents them from making decisions that affect the budget. In this case, the key operational decisions are made elsewhere in the organization, typically in the regional or state central offices that manage a series of individual DMV branch offices. It is at that level that Theory Y budgeting practices should apply, not at the individual branch office level.

The same situation applies to road crews, where the crew leader is a front-line supervisor but doesn't have much authority over other expenses; or firefighter shifts supervised by a battalion chief; mail carriers supervised by the local postmaster; or college professors supervised by a department chair. These front-line supervisors typically have little control over decisions that affect the budget. In the private sector, the same is true of large banks: the vice president who manages the local branch usually has very little control over office lease costs, the choice of Internet service provider, or even advertising.

A separate management question is this: *should* operational decisions be allowed to be made closer to the actual point of service delivery? If DMV or post offices are models of efficiency and citizen service, then the current level of operating control is appropriate. If not, then one strategy might be to empower the front line supervisor and his or her staff with more responsibility and authority over operating decisions that do affect the budget. Much of the recent research on quality and performance improvement suggests that this is a good idea.

Arguments for doing so include financial ones:

- An operating manager wondered why office paper procured by the central purchasing office cost significantly more than the paper sold to the general public by the warehouse store.
- A librarian discovered he could buy hardcover bestsellers cheaper at Costco than those obtained by the purchasing office.
- The Forest Supervisor knew she could save $18,000 per year in Internet costs by using the local municipal ISP, but the GSA insisted on using the regional phone monopoly.

For governments (and corporate bureaucracies), one of the greatest barriers to giving front line units more autonomy is the insistence on uniform levels of service. The weak link principle means, in practice, that this is uniformly mediocre service. If the residents of Shelbyville get particularly excellent service from their DMV office, the residents of Springfield might protest if they don't get the same. They won't protest, however, if Shelbyville's service is just as dismal as theirs. There probably isn't a simple solution to this problem; as H.L. Mencken said, "Democracy is the theory that the common people know what they want, and deserve to get it good and hard."

Another barrier is the simple fact that not all of us are good at managing budgets; in fact, if one considers the level of personal debt in the U.S., it seems very few of us are. This problem is addressed in the next section.

Can Operating Managers Really Manage Budgets?

The supervisor of the police patrol function typically gets to that position due to his or her knowledge of policing practices, and skill in communicating and in supervising staff. The same is true of a high school principal who is expected to combine a solid understanding of educational theory with good leadership skills. If they have general management skills (strategic planning, performance management, budget management, etc.), it is only because they somehow picked them up along the way. Even at the level of police chief or school superintendent, technical knowledge is given far greater weight than formal management education (for a police chief, graduation from the FBI academy is the pinnacle of educational achievement; for a school superintendent, it is a doctorate in education, not a professional degree in public or business administration).

But police patrol officers and school teachers together account for a huge share of local tax expenditures. Why is it that we assume the police patrol commander or the school principal should be excellent leaders of their staff, but not be competent in making budget decisions?

Part of the answer is an assumption that not all leaders of people are good at financial management. There is truth to this; many police commanders and school principals, earning six-figure salaries, do not know how to calculate a percentage increase in a quantity that varies over time. Responsibility for budget decisions should thus be limited to individuals who have either specific training or natural talent in working with numbers. They're the ones who are good at trend analysis and forecasting, efficiency improvements and time-and-motion studies, benchmarking and performance measurement, and best practices in purchasing and contracting.

The problem with this theory is that we can all list examples where the supposed experts in budgeting and finance have made absolutely bone-headed decisions. This is especially true in large bureaucracies, whether private or public. By far the most common reaction to major organizational budget decisions—especially those done in response to some perceived crisis—by those working in the trenches is WTF??"[50]

Another argument is that leadership is an art, a right brain activity, and financial management is a science, a left brain activity. People are born with one or the other skill, but not both. But if this is the case, why do we bother to *teach* knowledge and skills in both areas? Why would a school principal be expected to know the technical aspects of education, but not be able to *learn* the technical aspects of budgeting? Why would a police commander be expected to know the latest "best practice" in police procedures but be assumed to be incapable of learning how to manage financial resources?

It is a fair argument that few people are born into the world with an innate ability to manage a budget. But instead of accepting this situation and leaving budget management to (centralized) "experts," a Theory Y solution is to *train and educate* operating managers in budget management skills. It should be treated no differently than the need to train managers in effective supervision and motivation skills.

---

[50] An abbreviation for "I am surprised they made that particular decision."

Is Theory Y Budgeting Sustainable?

The innovations in the State of Minnesota's approach to budgeting described by Barzelay and by Osborne and Hutchinson were supported by the state's CEO in the late 1980s, Governor Rudy Perpich, an elected politician. Since then, the state has had four different CEOs: two professional politicians, a professional wrestler, and a lawyer. Has a Theory Y management philosophy survived?

The short answer seems to be "no." There are few apparent vestiges of the management philosophy that characterized Peter Hutchinson's days as Commissioner of Finance. There is still talk of the "price of government," but it seems to refer simply to the cost of various state services. A relatively new "pay for performance" program (mandated by state statute) is very much a Theory X system, consistent with Frederick Taylor's belief that employees, like trained mice, need to be rewarded with an external prize before they can be prodded to do good work.

Voters may rely on a variety of criteria to select their government's elected CEO, but it would be hard to argue that management skill is one of them. Professionals have a hard enough time hiring or promoting managers, using the best available tools of interviews, assessment centers, psychological testing, and reference checking. It would be unrealistic to expect voters to do any better. It is easy to picture the yawns and eye-rolling if a prospective politician-CEO actually started talking about delegation, motivation, values-oriented leadership, strategic planning and project management, especially when there are far more scintillating questions such as the candidate's stance on abortion or gay rights.

And a governor or mayor elected on a promise to turn things around would be expected to have a command-and-control management philosophy. How else would they bend the organization to their will, if not for a heroic centralized brute force management style? A patient, intentional approach to changing the organization's culture (typically requiring many years) simply does not sit well with a public that demands to see results early in a four-year term.

This would seem to ensure that any attempt toward a Theory Y management approach (by, say Governor Rudy Perpich or Vice President Al Gore) would be doomed to a short life. Governments run by politicians (the nation, states, and many large cities) could well be poor environments for an enlightened understanding of human psychology and an accompanying management self-discipline.

But by number, the majority of governments in the U.S., including most cities, and almost all special districts, are managed by CEOs who are professional managers (or at least selected by their boards on the assumption they fit this description). Their titles include city managers, school superintendents, and executive directors, among others. Many of them have actually studied the work of McGregor, Herzberg, and other management researchers, and have at least an intellectual understanding of the factors that motivate employees and managers. One would expect them to be more likely to initiate a Theory Y management approach (along with a complementary Theory Y budgeting system), and more likely to preserve and nurture one that already exists in an organization.

Indeed, after several decades, and some almost crippling budget challenges, the City of Fairfield still adheres to many of the key elements of Theory Y budgeting: tight alignment between the goals of the governing board and the budget decisions made by operating managers; a long-term (10-year) outlook; flexibility over line items; and carryover of savings. So does Chandler. In Visalia, California (the city Ted Gaebler managed and wrote about), the vestiges are more difficult to discern. But the city still uses a two-year budget, and departments still have flexibility over line items. So perhaps Theory Y budgeting has a better chance of survival in a professionally-managed government.

But governments with professional CEOs still show a high incidence of bureaucratic, rule-bound (Theory X) organizations. This could be because the Theory X culture is so ingrained in the organization that the CEO is powerless to change it. There is certainly truth in this. We will return to the central mystery of Theory Y budgeting ("why don't all governments do this?") in Chapter 8. Like a fungal infection, a Theory X culture, once established, might be very difficult to eradicate.

A more fundamental problem could be that most professional managers, at heart, are really Theory X managers. They may, on some theoretical level, acknowledge that their organization will perform best when their staff and managers are empowered to make their own decisions. But to actually manage and lead this way takes a leap of faith. The governing board, after all, holds the CEO personally responsible for organizational results. Micromanaging may be (in theory) bad, but it does allow the CEO to *control* the results. Trusting operating managers and their employees to make good decisions is a nice idea, but it makes the CEO vulnerable to the possibility of a screw up by dozens if not hundreds of human beings in the organization. A top-down centralized command-and-control system gives a (false) sense of security to the CEO.

The title of Herzberg's classic article, *One More Time: How Do You Motivate Employees?* reveals the author's frustration that managers who should know better continue to cling to a Theory X philosophy. How many times do we need to tell them that employees do their best work when they are empowered to make decisions for themselves? Why don't they get it? Even after all the good work by Maslow, Likert and others, managers still insisted on using what Herzberg called a KITA[51] approach to motivating employees. Why do that, he argued, when it is so much easier to have the employees *motivate themselves* by simply creating the right work environment?

When interviewing a city manager (or superintendent) candidate, a sophisticated city council (or school board) might well ask the question, "tell us about your management philosophy." The candidate will provide the correct answer: "I don't micromanage. I provide strong leadership but I believe in empowering my employees, and effective delegation. I hold employees accountable, but I believe they should have the resources to get the job done." And the candidate might well believe that this really is the way he or she manages. But as the saying goes, we judge ourselves by what we are capable of, and others judge us by what we do. It is the rare manager who really walks the talk. We can picture

---

[51] Translation: "Kick In The Ass"

the newly-hired city manager's first week on the job, when she is having her introductory meeting with the budget director:

"You really let departments carry over their savings?"

"Yep."

"How much?"

"Well, all of it."

"All of it! You mean you really let the fire chief have all that money? What keeps him from blowing it on the latest toys?"

"That wouldn't be consistent with council goals, so he doesn't do that."

"Yeah, right."

The budget director shrugs. "No, really."

"And someone said the budget workshop with the city council only lasts an hour. They were kidding, right?"

"No, that's about it. We give the departments targets based on council priorities, they stay within them, and the budget is balanced from the outset."

"But what if the department requests more? I bet the police department says, 'we don't need no stinkin' target.'"

"Requests? We don't have those. We just have targets. I know it seems strange—I've worked in other cities—but it's true."

"And you don't even review budget transfers?"

"Like what?"

"Like, if a department wants to spend some of their salary savings on a new pickup truck."

"Nope."

"Well, it sounds like your departments are running amok. That's one of the things I intend to fix."

What is the solution? Jim Collins and Jerry Porras suggest an answer in *Built to Last*.[52] They investigate organizations like Mayo Clinic, 3-M, and Hewlett-Packard that have been successful long after their founders have passed the baton of leadership. They find that key values of the organization ("patient first" for Mayo, innovation for 3-M) have been intentionally built into the DNA of the organization, to survive regardless of the individuals at the helm. These values are nurtured in a number of ways: in mission and value statements, in orientation (or "onboarding" to use the jargon de jour), and in the very language used by the organization. And new hires and promotions, *including* those for the CEO and top managers, are filtered according to these values. In fact, the organizations that are built to last have a higher tendency to promote from within, because this provides greater assurance that managers will buy into the foundational values.

A simple phrase that is often used by cities that have adopted Expenditure Control Budgeting is this: "we believe managers are paid to manage." It may seem to be a tautology, but the phrase is actually a very powerful and succinct statement of values. It at once emphasizes the *responsibility* of the manager in achieving the goals of the organization (and being accountable for results), while at the same time affirming that the manager should have the *authority* (and resources) to manage. It is in stark contrast to the (mercifully)

---

[52] Jim Collins & Jerry Porras, *Built to Last: Successful Habits of Visionary Companies* (Harper Business, 2004).

unwritten statement in rule-bound Theory X organizations: "we believe managers, like all other employees, are lazy and stupid, and need all these rules to keep from totally screwing up."

A principle that "managers are paid to manage" can be the kind of foundational value that Collins writes about. If applied intentionally and consistently to internal systems (personnel, purchasing, budgeting, and even to the process used to update the government's web site), it can be just as hard for a single (transitory) CEO to change as an ingrained Theory X philosophy.

The selection of a CEO does not occur in a vacuum. The managers who instill a Theory Y approach can manage upwards and continually remind the governing board that the organization is achieving results precisely because it gives its managers the responsibility and authority for managing. It is completely appropriate for the governing board to adopt this principle as one that will be followed by the organization. Even if board members know they should themselves exercise restraint in the internal management of the organization, it's a safe bet that the board of directors of 3-M buys into the value of innovation, and owns that value as a key factor in the long term success of the company. By the same token, the informal working environment of Google is a *corporate* value, not simply an internal policy.

The CEO hired or promoted by the governing board can have skills and experience that meet the unique needs of the organization for the times and environment it operates in. A school district facing severe fiscal constraints might hire a superintendent with strong financial skills, while a county experiencing rapid growth might hire an administrator with strong project management skills. But the governing board can and should insist that the CEO not only acknowledges, but embraces, the foundational values of the organization, including a Theory Y approach to management.

Effective Management In Spite of State Law

There is wide variation in state interference with the operations of local governments (the cities, counties, and special districts that make up the vast majority of governmental units and employees in the US). For a variety of reasons, the trend (nationwide) has been toward more restrictions on local authority, and a growing pile of state rules that limit how local governments operate.

These rules are often many decades behind the times, and have far outlived their relevance. For example, the State of Oregon's laws governing local government budgeting were written in an era when local governments could set their own property tax rates, when budget automation meant a typewriter and carbon paper, and newspapers were the only practical way to communicate with the public.

Further, state rules typically exhibit a strong Theory X bias, where all local government officials and staff are assumed to be not only lazy and stupid, but also sociopathic. Revenues are the province of treasurers and controllers, and if line managers even get near them, the primary issue is the creation of safeguards against embezzlement, not the role of the line manager in forecasting, or in enhancing the organization's ability to collect revenue. The profligate spenders on governing boards and staff must be kept on a short leash through appropriations laws, often requiring a convoluted process to amend appropriations when life inevitably doesn't proceed according to plans.

The obvious solution is to change the state laws, but state lawmakers typically have higher priorities, such as demonstrating they are tough on crime, or that they are serious about education. The fallback solution is to come up with creative ways to spend the minimum amount of staff time necessary to comply with the letter of the law, and to otherwise ignore state rules.

In the case of budgeting, this often requires maintaining two sets of books: one representing sound management, and the other representing the state's approach to management. The former includes revenues and beginning balances at the program level and a focus on the bottom line. The latter includes appropriations at whatever level the state deems necessary.

The line manager should be held accountable for the bottom line. If the building official spends more than was originally planned, then he or she should be able to show that revenues are likewise coming in higher than planned. That's all. The building official should not be encumbered with irrelevant distractions such as state-mandated appropriations. It should, instead, be the job of some staff support function (typically finance) to run interference for the line managers and simply take care of the state requirements. If that means cranking up a budget amendment process, so be it.

For this reason, local governments often accumulate budget amendments until the end of the fiscal period and process them all in one simple clean-up ordinance or resolution. If it doesn't require a public hearing, the action is placed on the governing body's consent agenda as a routine non-discussion item.

What About Contingency Theory?

According to contingency theory, there is no single best way to structure and manage an organization: organizational structure and management should instead be tailored to the environment the organization operates in. Gareth Morgan notes:[53]

- Organizations are open systems that need careful management to satisfy and balance internal needs and to adapt to environmental circumstances.
- There is no one best way of organizing. The appropriate form depends on the kind of task or environment one is dealing with.
- Management must be concerned, above all else, with achieving alignments and good fits.
- Different types or species of organizations are needed in different types of environments.

If contingency theory is right, there must be situations in which Theory Y budgeting is not appropriate. As noted above, first line supervisors in organizations that perform very routine and repetitive tasks might not need much responsibility over their budget because there is little that they can do to affect resources or spending. But the issue here is the appropriate *level* of the organization to assign budget authority and responsibility, not whether this authority will be

---

[53] Gareth Morgan, *Images of Organization* (Sage Publications, Inc, 2006).

delegated. There is, after all, an individual at *some* level of the organization (but below the CEO) whose decisions do affect revenues and expenditures.

The environments of different government organizations and agencies may differ substantially, but the nature of the people working in them does not change. Even though it may appear to the public that some agencies attract individuals who are lazy and stupid (we won't name names here), the reality is that people are wired pretty much the same, no matter the working environment they're in. This means that, regardless of the "technology" of the organization, or how open or fluid it is, people need to feel they have the resources they need to get the job done, they like to exercise control over their work, and they not only accept but seek responsibility. Under no circumstances do they do their best work in a mushroom-growing work environment (where they are kept in the dark and fed manure).

If the principles of Theory Y budgeting should be applied across different types of governmental organizations, should they also be applied at all times (i.e., in all circumstances)? Since this approach assumes a high degree of delegation and empowerment, it is well-suited to normal times, where challenges can be dealt with using ordinary tools and techniques. A more authoritative approach, however, might be called for when the organization is in crisis. And many governments are in crisis mode now, whether due to fiscal challenges, or political turmoil in their communities. Those organizations need a strong leader who can take command, right?

Wrong. Think about how we approach a natural disaster or emergency. The Incident Command System emphasizes a clear chain of command, and the importance of unambiguous decisions and direction. Sounds like a central command-and-control system. But what do professionals do when managing emergencies? They are clear about the outcomes they want to see, but *they give broad responsibility* to the people in the field as they achieve the outcomes. In an emergency, organizations actually *relax* purchasing requirements and other red tape. Incident commanders ask the field supervisors to tell them what they need to get their job done, and the commanders try to make sure they have it. They don't micromanage because they don't have the time to, and because they can't be in two places at one time. Instead of being authoritative, this is really a participative management approach, because executives leave it to the staff in the field to figure out for themselves how to get the job done. And as a result many of the people responding to an emergency find the work exhilarating, even in the face of tragedy.

This should tell us something. To respond best to a crisis, we should be clear about goals and expected outcomes, and establish clearly-defined areas of responsibility. Once that's done, we should make sure staff have the resources they need, and then get out of their way. If this works in a crisis, why don't we do this all the time? To be sure, in an emergency there might not be time to solicit multiple quotes for goods and services, and we would want to do this in more relaxed circumstances. But why in the world do we revert to micro managing budgets when a crisis is over?

A Theory Y budget system may well be compatible with any of the organizational structures that might be considered optimal under contingency theory. For example, a common question is whether to organize by program (or product or

THE HUMAN SIDE OF BUDGETING

service), or function. If organized by program, the police and public works departments include their own accounting, HR, IT, and purchasing staffs. If organized by function, accountants are centralized in their own department, as are each of the professional disciplines that support the organization. There are trade-offs in each approach, and it isn't uncommon for the two types of structure to swing like a pendulum through large organizations (staff functions are centralized to avoid duplication and increase coordination, then the staff functions become bloated and unresponsive so the staff are spun off to the line departments, and the cycle begins again).

Theory Y budgeting works under either structure. Once an organizational unit (of any kind) is formed, and a manager is given responsibility for managing that unit, then the manager should have as much control as possible over the budget and other resources available to that unit. It really doesn't make much difference whether the manager is providing direct service to citizens, or providing service to other departments.

Another issue is the degree of openness or flexibility of the organization. In a stable environment with routine activities, an organization might have a fairly rigid (and traditional) structure, with clear and relatively stable lines of authority. But in an environment with a high degree of change and uncertainty, the organizational structure may be more fluid, with a series of ad-hoc cross-functional work teams that quickly form and disband as needed.

There is no question that Theory Y budgeting works in "traditional" organizational structures: it's the arrangement used by most cities (and states) that have tried it. Some aspects of the system work especially well in this environment. Carryover of year-end savings, for example, makes most sense when the same organizational unit will continue to function from year to year. It is less of an issue for a project team that might only exist for three weeks or months.

But consider other aspects of Theory Y budgeting in a fluid, or open, organizational environment:

- <u>Budget targets</u>. This is probably the only logical way to allocate financial resources. The typical budget request circus only works when all budgets can be set in lockstep for all organizational units for the same budget cycle. Not all ad-hoc work teams have (or need) financial resources beyond their own staff time, but if they do, someone in the organization needs to give them an overall bottom line budget.

- <u>Control over line items.</u> Line item budgets are still useful in fluid environments: they are probably the best way to estimate the amount of resources necessary for a project or team. But they should be used for estimates only, and not as an arbitrary control over spending.

- <u>Bottom-line budget management</u>. A project team should be responsible for managing the net use of the organizations resources, or total costs less any project revenues.

Conclusion

This chapter begins with a Yogi Berra quote, and it's appropriate to end with another one:

THE HUMAN SIDE OF BUDGETING

"When you come to a fork in the road, take it."

Moving from a Theory X to a Theory Y budgeting system does require some critical decisions on what the new rules will be, how they will be applied, and who will be allowed to play the game. There will be forks in the road, and choices over which fork to take. Here are some thoughts on how to make these choices.

Computers have become powerful tools for solving complex equations. They do it using brute force and trial-and-error to home in on the solution. Using a simple example, to find the vertex of the parabola described by $y = -2(x)^2 + 20x + 200$, the starting point in a trial-and-error solution might be 100. The computer could try moving in small increments—say, 101, then 99—to discover that moving to the left along the x-axis gets closer to the maximum (the vertex). But continuing to move in similar small increments would require another 95 calculations to reach the correct answer of five.

But if the computer intentionally overshoots—say by first trying 100 and then trying negative 100, then 0, then 50, etc.—it would arrive at the correct answer in just a dozen or so calculations. Design engineers use the same principle: it's usually best to test the extremes and bracket the solution than to move incrementally (and slowly) toward a solution.

By the same token, the normal tendency in moving from a Theory X system to a Theory Y one is to do it cautiously and incrementally, but that would be wrong. It's better to take the forks in the road that test the extremes:

- Give operating managers as much control as possible over their resources

- Push budget control as far as far down the organization as possible (or to put it a better way, to the level of the individual teams and project groups)
- Assume that all staff can be trained and trusted to manage financial resources
- Assume that all staff are motivated by a desire to serve the public, and they look to the guidance of the elected governing body in setting priorities for programs and services.

The reason this is better than an incremental approach is that there are always strong reactive forces that try to push systems back to a Theory X state. An incremental approach will simply be exhausting for the organization's leaders who are trying to build empowering and self-regulating systems, and an approach that is too cautious will almost certainly fall far short of its potential.

If a radical change conjures up images of *Public Managers Gone Wild,* the actual experience of governments that have tried it is that operating managers are fairly timid in testing their newfound freedom. Martin Seligman, author of *Learned Optimism,* found that dogs that had been caged for a long time learned helplessness. When their cage walls were lowered— even when they received a mild shock—they had just "lain down whimpering."[54] People learn helplessness, too, and the challenge in moving to a Theory Y system is not that managers will go wild and abuse their new freedom, but that they will be too hesitant in doing so.

---

[54] Martin E. Seligman, *Learned Optimism: How to Change Your Mind and Your Life* (Knopf, 1991), Kindle location 550.

8

WHY DON'T ALL GOVERNMENTS DO IT THIS WAY?

A Theory Y approach to budgeting works: managers *do* make good decisions; they are creative; and they manage their resources well. More important, it brings the budget process into alignment with a management philosophy that acknowledges that employees are thinking, caring people who are naturally motivated to do good work. After fifty years of research, this philosophy is not just a matter of style—it reflects the way human beings are actually wired.

So we return to the question: why don't more governments do it this way? There are many possible reasons. Some have to do with the individuals leading the organization. Some have to do with the other systems and institutions within the organization. And some have to do with the "owners" of the government—the citizens—and their elected representatives. The suggestions put forth in this chapter are hypotheses, but they are based on over three decades of experience and study of governmental budget systems.

Failure to Walk the Talk

As noted in the previous chapter, some CEOs of governmental organizations may have (through training) learned to say the right things about delegation and empowering employees, but in their heart of hearts, they don't believe it. They may know at some intellectual level that they should trust their staff, and relinquish control over most resource decisions to the operating managers…but they just can't bring themselves to do it. They are, after all, the one ultimately accountable.

In an organization, "passing the buck," happens when individuals or departments try to shift responsibility for action (or blame) to someone else, or to another part of the organization. President Harry Truman famously had a sign on his desk that read, "the buck stops here." A nice image, but Harry Truman was the CEO of an organization of over two million federal employees (more than today, counter to popular perception)and it was not humanly possible to control (or even influence) the decisions of a small fraction of that number. Still, we cling to the image of the CEO as a take-charge person with his or her finger on the pulse (if not more intimate body parts) of the organization.

It may be an occupational hazard: organizations may tend to choose Theory X command-and-control individuals for their top executives, or people with those tendencies may be drawn to the role. Management consultant David Baker observes, "After interviewing more than 10,000 employees at

600+ companies, you start noticing patterns in management...One of the most fascinating to me is the overwhelming presence of control freaks."[55]

Enlightened CEOs, even if they are wired to be "control freaks", understand the truth of the quote from Tom Peters in Chapter 3: "Increased spending authority does not entail a loss of control. To the contrary, it begets more control of the most powerful sort—self-control." If entrusting operating managers with control over their resources is a leap of faith, control freaks can feed their compulsion by doing the following:

1. Ensure that operating managers are well-trained in managing their budgets.

2. Set clear and specific financial policies (as long as they are obviously tied to the financial health of the organization, and not rules for rules' sake). As noted earlier, it would be fiscally prudent, for example, to limit the use of one-time carryover savings to one-time expenses.

3. Establish efficient but effective monitoring systems so first, the operating managers know exactly how their units are performing, and second, so the executive leadership of the organization have real-time, high-level information on the overall financial health of the organization. (More on this in the next session).

---

[55]David Baker, Innovation & Strategy Blog, http://ldrlb.co/2012/01/control-freaks-in-management/ accessed on 8/31/12.

Getting Bad Advice

I used to think the brain was the most important organ in the body, then I realized —- look what's telling me that.–Emo Phillips

Only a fraction of the top managers in governmental organizations have a strong background in budgeting and finance. Those who don't often (appropriately) seek the advice of experts in the organization when establishing or changing budget systems. Even more often (and not so appropriate), the executive leaders leave the whole system to the "experts," obediently playing their prescribed roles (i.e., presiding over the budget request games, presenting the budget assembled by the experts to the governing board) on cue.

Who are those experts? They tend to be accountants, housed in the finance, accounting, or treasury departments. Or they may be central budget analysts, who may not be CPAs but still have a strong affinity for numbers.

And they probably are characterized by personality types that complement that of the CEO.

For example, a commonly-used measure of personality is the Myers-Briggs Type Indicator. While it is an over-generalization, organization leaders might tend to fall into a "ENFP" Myers-Briggs quadrant, representing the type indicators of extroversion, intuition, feeling, and perception. These leaders, if they are good, will recognize they need people in the organization who have different personality types, to provide a healthy balance and to compensate for their own blind spots. While it is also an over-generalization, finance staff members might fall into the ISTJ quadrant, representing the type indicators of introversion, sensing, thinking, and judging. People with the ISTJ type indicators like order, and are drawn to careers in the military and law, as well as accounting. And it is good for an organization to have the folks counting and tracking money to be detail-oriented, careful, with a strong affinity for rules and facts.

The problem occurs when these people are asked to design management systems. It should be no surprise that a budget process designed by accountants will be one that is heavy on rules, and one that gives the finance director (or budget director) a major role in making budget decisions for the organization. Indeed, the Government Finance Officers Association has developed "best practices" for budget systems that include these elements:

A government should develop, review, improve, and implement strategies that encourage the organization and its employees to work toward achievement of goals. These strategies include both positive *incentives and penalties.*

Mechanisms should be in place to detect and correct deviations from the budget. These measures may be as simple as a requirement (supported by appropriate *rewards and penalties*) that managers not go over budget. Budgetary compliance is encouraged through use of data collection and reporting systems that *control* disbursements of funds...Mechanisms usually also include the assignment of budget or finance personnel to conduct monthly or quarterly reviews of trends in actual expenditures and revenues and actual-to-budget comparisons so that timely *corrective action* can be taken.

In developing budget guidelines and instructions, a government should consider the role played by the various stakeholders such as *departments within the government* or other agencies that are involved in budget preparation. Involving stakeholders may be accomplished by holding meetings in which administrative staff and selected internal and external stakeholders help develop the processes and general directions provided to budget preparers. Given time and resource constraints, full stakeholder input may not be practical.[56]

These "best practices" are dominated by a central command-and-control approach to budget management. It is the (central) finance and budget personnel who watch revenue and spending trends to ensure that "timely corrective action can be taken." The operating managers are relegated to the status of mere "stakeholders," and a good way to involve these stakeholders is holding meetings with them. The chorus of calls for rewards and punishments for operating managers and other employees could not have been better sung by Frederick Taylor himself.

If you made the observation that these practices seem to assume operating managers will tend to be lazy, stupid, and conniving, their response would be, "Yes. What's the question?" Their entire reason for being is to serve as the

---

[56]GFOA web site, http://www.gfoa.org/services/nacslb/ accessed on 10/27/12. Emphasis added.

bulwark against corruption, waste, inefficiency, and poor judgment, all committed by other people in the organization. A system that empowers mere mortals with significant authority over resource decisions would be completely unnatural, like breathing under water.

Edwin Caplan, in an examination of the behavioral assumptions of management accounting (including budget systems), confirms that the world view of accountants is firmly in the "traditional" world of Taylorism, where management must "control the tendencies of employees to be lazy, wasteful, and inefficient."[57] Caplan contrasts this with "modern" organization theory proposed by McGregor and others that refutes the principles of scientific management. Nonetheless, "there has been a single view of human behavior [the traditional scientific management view] in business organizations from the period of the industrial revolution to the present and...management accounting has adopted this view without significant modification or serious question as to its validity."[58]

Even if a CEO were intrigued with something like Expenditure Control Budgeting, where operating units are allowed to keep carryover savings, the finance/budget czar could come up with a long list of objections. Why should we reward managers when they just get lucky and get more revenue than they estimated? They aren't qualified to manage money, and they don't have the aptitude to learn it. They're too busy running their departments to spend time on

---

[57]Edwin H. Caplan, "Behavioral Assumptions of Management Accounting" in *Public Budgeting and Finance,* Robert Golembiewski and Jack Rabin, eds., Marcel Dekker, New York, 1983, p.46.
[58]Ibid., p. 51.

financial trend analysis. They're only in it for themselves; they don't see the big picture. It's inefficient; our staff can put together a spreadsheet in a fraction of the time of those amateurs. We would lose control over our finances and face certain doom. We can't make good decisions on investing the city's cash if we don't control cash flow. Hardly any other governments do it this way and even big businesses keep their departments on a short budget leash. The audit firm will raise objections in its management letter. Bond rating agencies will lower our rating and we won't be able to sell bonds. This flies in the face of time-tested best practices that have been supported by GFOA. And so on.

In a large organization, these and other objections will be raised by in unison by a strong coalition of experts: the chief accountant, the budget director, the controller, the internal auditor, and the treasurer. This coalition will get moral support from like-minded directors of other staff agencies: the HR director, IT director, legal counsel, purchasing agent, and possibly even the city engineer and building official.

In the face of such unified objection from people who are paid to know this stuff, it would be no surprise that a well-intentioned CEO would begin to have serious doubts about the wisdom of trying a radically different approach to budget management.

Admittedly, this characterization of finance experts is a gross over-generalization. Some (if not many) in fact combine a command of finance with an appreciation (naturally-acquired, or through education) of human psychology and human relations. They can be excellent leaders and managers, skilled at applying Tom Peters' "loose-tight" principle in balancing the need for financial controls with the need to empower managers and employees. The individual credited with inventing Expenditure Control Budgeting was himself an assistant finance director and former banker. The budget directors and finance directors of cities like Fairfield, California and Chandler, Arizona have been among the strongest proponents of Theory Y approaches to budget management.

But it would be hard to argue that these people are not the exception to the rule. Rather than attempting to pound a square peg into a round hole (i.e., asking finance experts to design good management systems), a much better approach is to apply the skills of the financial experts in the areas where they can best benefit the organization.[59] In fact, their role in a Theory Y budget system is absolutely critical, and includes the following:

- Helping to train operating managers in analyzing and interpreting financial reports, and in budget forecasting and estimating. Ideally, this is done in partnership with people skilled at educating adults (sometimes found in HR departments)
- Establishing high-level policies, such as the appropriate use of one-time resources (the rules should, however, be kept to an absolute minimum)
- Providing easy-to-understand real-time reports on financial performance for operating managers (heeding Drucker's advice in Chapter 2 that the

---

[59] Marcus Buckingham & Curt Coffman, *First, Break All the Rules: What the World's Greatest Managers Do Differently* (Simon & Schuster, 1999).

detailed reports go directly to the operating managers rather than to their supervisors)

- Providing summary reporting at the appropriate levels of the organization. If department heads are given responsibility (and accountability) over the bottom-line performance of their departments, then the CEO should get periodic reports on the bottom line performance of the departments. And department heads should get summary reports on the bottom line performance of their program managers.

- Developing and monitoring early warning signals for the organization. Treasurers are typically in a good position to do this, since they are the first to see trends in the cash position of the organization. There are often good reasons to spend down cash (e.g., to construct a bond-funded building or bridge), but no organization should ever be caught by surprise by inadvertently spending beyond its means. Theory Y (decentralized) budgeting actually helps avoid surprises (there are many fingers on the financial pulse of the organization, and many people with a stake in sound financial management). But as a practical matter, governments with major tax sources such as property, income, or sales tax need to have someone good at forecasting these sources. And on the expenditure side, some central analyst needs to forecast trends in pension and health benefit costs that affect multiple programs.

- *Advising* operating managers on ways to cut costs and increase revenues. Research and performance measurement units can be set up as internal consulting organizations, but only as long as operating managers are free to take or leave their service (and pay for it on a voluntary basis).[60]

This role for finance experts can actually improve their job satisfaction. Instead of constantly fighting operating managers, when they switch to a role of teaching, advising, and supporting *at the request* of the operating managers, they can earn newfound respect in the organization and are treated as critical team members in fulfilling the higher purpose of serving citizens and customers.

Patching an Old Garment With New Cloth

Many bureaucracies are thoroughly infected by Theory X systems and processes. The budget system is just the tip of the iceberg. Personnel, or human resources, systems are notoriously dysfunctional. Trial lawyers have prompted the creation of a pile of case law that treats all managers as sadists and all employees as sociopaths. It's no secret why we do annual performance evaluations: it is to send the clear message to our staff that "we really value you, and you're doing a great job...but I have to document your every flaw because some day I may want to fire you." This is insane.

Scott Adams in his *Dilbert* comic strip has created the character, "Mordac the Preventer of Information Systems." It resonates with readers since we have all come across IT directors who seem to take perverse pleasure in supplying operating departments with outdated software and

---

[60] See again Pinchot & Pinchot, *The End of Bureaucracy.*

technology, or in denying access to computers.[61]

Purchasing agents and buyers lord over the operating departments their power in rejecting requisitions, and substituting their judgment for that of their internal customers. Legal departments take six months to approve a one-page contract; HR departments drag out a hiring process and then provide a short list of applicants who really aren't qualified for the job. The webmaster is the only one allowed to make changes to the web site, and by the time he or she gets around to updating it, the news is already outdated. Getting an action item in front of the governing council or board means running a gauntlet of approvals and reviews that seem to be intended to punish staff for bothering the CEO and board.

These are some of the "twisted pipe" systems described so well by Ken Miller. Changing the budget system without tackling these other internal processes sends the message, "we'll treat you as a thinking, caring human being in this area...but in no other." Operating managers would get a taste of freedom and then be subjected to the usual slavery to the internal staff masters. It would be a form of organizational schizophrenia.

And changing these systems is no simple task. Even with strong executive pressure to do so, the gatekeepers of the internal staff functions may sense a threat to their very existence, and counter with at least malicious obedience, if not outright rebellion. "We've always done it this way," to

---

[61] True story: when the author served as a budget director, the IT director refused to allow a team of budget analysts to purchase and share a laptop computer on the argument that the analysts might take the computer home and play games on it.

"this is counter to our industry's best practices" will be excuse for clinging to the status quo, which is always the easiest course.

But it can be done. The State of Minnesota apparently provided an example, if only a short-lived one. In many private organizations, the change has been more enduring, as documented by many management gurus, and supported by research on methods for changing organizational culture.

The Tyranny of Dead Ideas

The citizens often know what they want, and demand that governments give it to them. And they aren't encumbered by ends and means distinctions. *How* a service is delivered is just as (if not more) important than the service itself. And public pressure for certain approaches to service delivery and government administration is often based on an erroneous understanding of human psychology.

Matt Miller in *The Tyranny of Dead Ideas* argues that "from the halls of government to the executive suite, from the corner store to the factory floor, Americans are in the grip of a set of ideas that are not only dubious or dead wrong— they're on a collision course with social and economic developments that are now irreversible." Miller focuses on "dead ideas" that work against solutions to broad economic and societal challenges, but the same observation can be made about management systems.

Consider, for example, the public clamoring for pay-for-performance systems for teachers as the solution to the dismal state of U.S. secondary education. The assumption here is that teachers generally choose to be ineffective, but a financial reward is all it takes for them to choose to be effective. This Pavlovian view of reward and punishment as the primary driver of quality work has, as noted earlier, been refuted by decades of research on work motivation, but it is still widely held by the public in general, and many of the elected officials who represent them.

By the same token, the Theory X assumption that employees, if left to their own devices, will tend to be lazy and stupid (and unethical) appears to be a popular belief, even if citizens would object to these descriptions being applied to *them*. Indeed, the trends in government finance that have been strongly supported by voters are completely consistent with a Theory X philosophy. These include increased restrictions applied to the use of taxes and other revenue sources, a shift in taxes and service provision from general purpose governments to special purpose districts, and the creation of internal auditor positions (sometimes directly elected).

In this environment, delegating budget authority to operating managers, and giving them more authority (and responsibility) over their financial resources would seem to be having the fox guard the henhouse. The "waste and abuse" that, according to popular political discourse, is so rampant in government must be due to the profligate spending of operating managers and their employees. The possibility that waste, where it does exist, might be due to the silly rules and useless procedures that managers are subjected to would never occur to the average person in the street.

In our representative democracy, it is no accident that elected officials often mirror the beliefs and biases of the public at large. If gaining results by relinquishing control seems difficult for the "control freak" CEOs (even if they know, intellectually, that it's the right thing to do), how much more difficult it is to swallow by members of elected governing boards.

Conclusion

To a reader interested in exploring Theory Y budgeting, this chapter may seem discouraging. In any organization, it could well be an uphill battle. But we should not expect that good management (and an evidence-based understanding of human relations) is the natural state of organizations. Just as many aspects of our complex human civilization take effort to work against the second law of thermodynamics, it takes effort to manage well. Management consultant David Horsager exhorts us to "stop being lazy and do the right thing."[62] Effective management takes discipline and perseverance.

The point is that the fact that a relatively small number of governments have adopted elements of Theory Y budgeting is *not* evidence that it is ineffective or represents poor financial management. It may, instead, reflect the tyranny of the dead ideas of Taylorism and a Theory X philosophy of management.

---

[62] David Horsager, *The Trust Edge: How Top Leaders Gain Faster Results, Deeper Relationships, and a Stronger Bottom Line*, Free Press (2012).

9

CURRENT AND FUTURE RESEARCH

A literature search reveals very little scholarly discussion of the elements of Theory Y budgeting. In fact, examination of the relationship between budget systems and human behavior is rare. Robert Golembieski and Jack Rabin explore the topic in their *Public Budgeting and Finance: Behavioral, Theoretical and Technical Perspectives*. A chapter by Edwin Caplan, as noted earlier, shows that management accounting systems are based on the traditional scientific management assumptions of human behavior. Another chapter, by Roger Blakeney, contrasts the "classical" theory with the more recent work by Maslow, McGregor, and Herzberg,[63] but it makes no suggestions on how budget systems might be modified in light of this research on motivation.

A few articles on Expenditure Control Budgeting appeared in academic journals in the early 1990s, following publication of Osborne and Gaebler's *Reinventing Government* and around the same time as the national government reform

---

[63] Roger N. Blakeney, "Motivation Theories," in *Public Budgeting and Finance*, Robert Golembiewski and Jack Rabin, eds., Marcel Dekker, New York, 1983, pp. 125-138.

efforts of the Clinton administration. Since then, attention has returned to where it has always been: on the budget *policy* process, not on the function of the budget as a management tool. This is possibly because the field of public administration has been overrun by political scientists,[64] and because the policy battles are, frankly, more interesting.

Eric Herzik, in his 1991 article on ECB, notes that the small number of governments that had (at that time) adopted the new budget philosophy would make it difficult to perform a rigorous analysis of its effectiveness.[65]The small "N," combined with methodological problems in measuring the output (quantity *and* quality) of governmental services, would make it difficult to isolate the effect of ECB on "agency efficiency."[66]

Actually, the research problem is even more challenging. Theory Y budgeting is not so much a financial tool as a way to bring budget management into alignment with an overall (Theory Y) management philosophy. As noted previously, introducing expenditure control budgeting, or something like it, in a typical Theory X organization could be worse than futile since it would send mixed (and contradictory) messages to the operating managers and their staff.

And under some circumstances, a typical Theory X budget process in the midst of an otherwise Theory Y organization could still yield some efficiencies. The price of a dysfunctional organization is not always revealed in the ratio of outputs to inputs. Many organizations do a good job of

[64] David L. Weimer, "Political Science, Practitioner Skill, and Public Management," *Public Administration Review*, 52 (3), pp. 240-245.
[65]Herzik op cit.
[66] Op cit. p. 246

doing the wrong thing very efficiently; just think of airlines that cram passengers like cattle into their planes, DMV offices, or cable TV installers. A cross-sectional analysis of organizations that do and do not use Theory Y budget processes could well yield inconclusive *financial* results.

But this does not mean that Theory Y budgeting should not be put to the test. A well-managed organization must, after all, be more effective by *some* measure if it can truly claim to be well-managed. The trick is to come up with a robust measure of the overall effectiveness of a government. The management literature bulges with studies of the effect of different leadership and management practices on the effectiveness of for-profit corporations, using measures such as return on stockholder equity.[67] There is no similar literature for governments, due at least partly to the difficulty in coming up with similar measures of the effectiveness of public (or nonprofit) organizations.[68]

The typical cross sectional study would suffer from a small sample size and too many independent variables. An alternative might be to set up experimental simulations of government organizations, testing the following four scenarios:

---

[67] See, for example, Jim Collins & Morten Hansen, *Great By Choice,* Harper Collins, 2011.

[68] And possibly also due to the relative lack of attention to leadership and management issues by the public administration field as compared to the business administration field.

	Theory X Budget Systems	Theory Y Budget Systems
Theory X Organization	A	B
Theory Y Organization	C	D

The hypothesis is that a Theory Y budget system embedded in an overall Theory Y organization (scenario D in the table) would yield the most effective organization, where effectiveness might be measured by such factors as:

- Ability of the organization to respond quickly to abrupt changes in the environment;
- Resilience of the organization to external and internal challenges;
- Adoption of creative or innovative solutions to problems;
- Alignment of the activities and output of the organization with the priorities of the governing board;
- Job satisfaction of employees.

A case study approach might also be helpful, using longitudinal studies of governments before and after moving to Theory Y management systems from Theory X management systems (and vice versa), using the same effectiveness measures noted above. Although this would be a qualitative, rather than quantitative, analysis, it would suffer from the same problem of too many changes in independent variables (political and demographic changes in the community, turnover of staff, changes in economic conditions, changes in mandates and preemptions from higher levels of government, etc.).

10

BEYOND BUDGETING

There is a small but growing movement in the private sector, beginning with some European companies, but spreading to some US ones as well, that questions the very notion of a budget itself. Circumstances change so quickly in the current Information Age, the argument goes, that being locked into the traditional annual budget plan can harm rather than help an organization respond appropriately to fast-moving challenges and opportunities.

The alternative is not merely to stop budgeting, but to *replace* a fixed budget cycle with the following kinds of elements:

- A rolling forecast (e.g., on a five-year horizon) updated fairly frequently (e.g., quarterly) that puts the organization's current financial picture in context with a longer view of financial and market trends. This also allows the organization to test the effect of current decisions on the long term health of the organization, under varying assumptions about the future (in line with the "productive paranoia" that Collins and Hansen associate with great organizations[69]).

- Key performance indicators—for example, return-on-capital, net cash flow, cost-to-income ratio—rather than fixed spending amounts, and an emphasis on outcomes that further the organization's goals.

- Allocation of the firm's (central) resources through fast-track approvals of seed money or investments in new ventures on an as-needed basis rather than according to some fixed and arbitrary calendar date.

- Accurate snapshots of the financial health of the organization provided in real time via modern computer-based finance systems, no matter how large and far-flung the organization. The focus is on trends and forecasts rather than the "rear view mirror."[70]

While these elements are a response to the shortcomings of traditional budgeting by corporations, governments share some frustration with the budget process. No matter how we dress it up, few citizens actually show up for budget hearings.[71] To the few who do participate, the final budget seems to be a foregone conclusion, and the governing body appears to simply rubber-stamp the budget brought forward

---

[69]Collins & Merton, *Great by Choice.*
[70]Jeremy Hope & Robin Fraser, *Beyond Budgeting,* Harvard Business School Press, Boston, 2003.
[71]Jonathan Walters, "O Citizen Where Art Thou?" *Governing,* April, 2009.

by the CEO. There may be controversy and a spirited political discussion around some element of the budget, but it usually amounts to only a small percentage of total spending (e.g., federal funding of National Public Radio).

The vast majority of a budget is simply the result of a series of policy decisions that have been made in the past. Employee pension rates are set by an actuarial analysis based on past benefit promises, and employee pay scales and health benefits are set by union contracts. A decision to build a new fire station, school, or swimming pool locks the government into inescapable operating costs. Long term agreements set the wholesale cost of water, and lease-purchase agreements set the cost of street sweepers and fire pumpers. Federal and state mandates determine the costs of social services and sewage permit fees.

In some cases, these decisions are made concurrently with the annual budget; usually they are not. Sometimes the long term consequences on the operating budget of major capital improvements are explicitly addressed when the capital decisions are made; all too often they are not, in spite of a century of doing annual budgets.

Against this reality, the concepts underlying the "beyond budgeting" movement make some sense. The operating costs of a building or other public facility shouldn't be ignored until some future annual budget process comes around (when the facility comes on line); they should instead be fed into the rolling forecast to make sure they will be sustainable. Self-supporting operations make up an increasing share of state and local expenditures in our current tax-adverse environment (and one in which taxes, when they are approved, are increasingly limited to very specific services).

The bottom-line approach here is clearly a useful one: the direction from the governing board and CEO to the operating managers is "squeeze the most service possible from your available revenue, and otherwise don't bother us." Decisions on the use of general revenues or cash balances as a grant match must be made when the grant opportunity comes up; budgeting for competitive grants in an annual process is always a (pointless) crapshoot. And real-time financial indicators should prompt an immediate reaction when it appears the organization is heading for a financial cliff; waiting until the beginning of the next budget cycle only compounds the problem.

Most of these ideas would be difficult or impossible to implement in a traditional Theory X budgeting system. In these, there is only a tenuous and indirect link to financial reality. A projection of available revenue is made well in advance of the beginning of the next fiscal year (sometimes as many as 18 months in advance). From that point on, the budget takes on a life of its own in a sort of parallel universe. The revenue projection sets the amount of the budget, and it leads to a zero-sum game in the struggle to see who gets the (projected) money. The only thing that matters to the operating manager is the *appropriation* for the department or program, which is often broken down into budget limits for individual line items or categories of line items, and allotments that limit spending by quarter or month. Managers are held accountable for spending in relation to the budget, and sanctions (forms of punishment) for spending that exceeds the budget limit. This parallel universe (as seen by the operating manager) is completely separate from the actual bottom-line financial performance of the organization, and separate from issues of quality and quantity of service.

Someone in a Theory X system is paying attention to the net financial performance of the organization, but it is some central staff person, not the operating managers. If revenues come in higher than the budget projection, it means the following year's budget process will be a little easier. If they come in lower than projected, the central finance staff usually have some amount of fund balance squirreled away that absorbs the drop in revenue. The annual financial report will show that the organization didn't perform, overall, as well as expected, but this financial report typically doesn't come out until six months *after* the fiscal year has ended, and no one really cares about it at that point. The annual report also fixates on spending compared to the *budgeted* (or planned) amounts of spending. The real picture of financial performance is buried in statements of "revenues, expenditures, and changes in fund balance," and governing bodies rarely know what to do with them. These statements are shown at the fund level, as they must be because revenues are usually lumped in one place for the entire fund. Therefore it is impossible to hold anyone accountable for bottom line financial performance since no one is really responsible for it.

On the other hand, a Theory Y budgeting system could provide a good platform for venturing into a "beyond budgeting" approach. It already incorporates bottom-line financial management at the operating unit level, where operating managers are responsible for dealing with both estimated and actual revenues, and managing actual expenditures in relation to actual revenues. The ability to carry over savings provides a built-in source of funding for one-time investments in equipment or projects. As in the "beyond budgeting" corporations, there is still a role for central management in setting overall targets and allocating, when needed, additional funds as seed money for new programs or major investments in equipment or capital improvements.

The only major change would be to shift from a biennial (or annual) budget to the rolling long range forecast as the primary platform for evaluating the financial implications of policy changes. It takes the change from an annual Theory X budget to a biennial Theory Y budget one step further, by lengthening the time period covered by the projections (for example, from two years to five years) and by increasing the frequency with which the projections are updated (for example, from once every one or two years to quarterly).

This could be a major improvement, on both the revenue side and the expenditure side. Some revenues, such as property taxes or business license renewals, follow an annual cycle, but most do not. Once rates are set, income and sales taxes rise and fall with changes in the underlying income and sales bases, and while there may be seasonal patterns that appear on a twelve-month cycle, there is no reason to pick one date over another as the beginning of the cycle. Local and state governments that receive federal grant revenue typically use different fiscal years than the federal October 1- September 30 year, and it has become rare for the federal budget to be adopted at the start of its fiscal year anyway.

On the expenditure side, employee health care and liability insurance premium amounts may be set on an annual basis, but not necessarily in line with the beginning of the government's fiscal year. Other expenses, such as utilities, may vary seasonally, but rate increases almost never correspond with the beginning of a fiscal year. It is not at all unusual for labor contract negotiations to extend well into a new fiscal year, long after the formal budget has been set.

Another advantage is that forecasts, even simple ones, typically include a set of explicitly-stated underlying assumptions on factors such as inflation rates, growth in population or customers, etc. These assumptions can be updated fairly easily as economic and demographic conditions change, and they can indicate how sensitive the organization's financial health is to changes in these factors. In contrast, a one- or two-year budget is based on many different assumptions on future conditions, but once the budget is adopted, there is no easy way to untangle the independent variables (economics, demographics, external cost and revenue factors) from the dependent variables (the final estimated revenues and appropriations).

The following table summarizes the differences between a typical Theory X budget, and Theory Y budget, and a "Beyond" budget process.

	Theory X	Theory Y	Beyond Budgeting
Planning period	Annual budget	Biennial (or annual) budget	Long range (e.g., 5-year) rolling forecast
Level of control	Appropriations (spending limits)	Bottom line: net share of general revenues, if any	Same as Theory Y
When major policy shifts are made	During annual budget	During budget process	Whenever needed (no set schedule)

It would be interesting to see some brave government (probably a local one) actually test the principles of the "beyond budgeting" movement. A possible objection to moving from a Theory Y budget to the next step "beyond" is that there would be no clearly-defined time for the governing board to make major policy changes. The board might worry that it could be left out of the fun of budgeting. But as noted above, few policy changes really line up neatly with the budget calendar. The kinds of events that might trigger a major governing board action or reaction include:

- A major swing in the political makeup of the board (e.g., a switch in the majority from conservative to liberal in a nonpartisan board or vice versa, or a switch in the majority party in a partisan board). This would most likely happen after a regular election, but it can also happen after a recall election in jurisdictions that give citizens the power of recall.
- A shock to the local economy, such as closure of a major factory or relocation of a corporate headquarters.
- A sudden, unexpected opportunity, such as the availability of a large piece of property or building, a major grant, a windfall from a court settlement, or formation of a new partnership with other public or private agencies.
- A major natural disaster.

Of these, only the first (an election that results in a major shift in composition of the governing board) provides a possibility for the budget calendar to be useful in causing a financial reaction to the change. And even here, due to the lag time in preparing budgets, newly-seated governing board members must often wait through a full budget cycle before they can have any real influence on financial priorities. In all other cases, a system that makes it easier to adjust financial priorities at any time would make the organization more responsive to the governing board's policy setting role, not less. Setting the direction of the organization (including the financial direction) would be a continuous function of the board, not just one it exercises every 12 or 24 months.

Another objection could be a legal requirement to have

an adopted budget (federal law applies this requirement to private nonprofit corporations; state law typically applies it to local governments as well as to the state itself). But this is a very simple problem to solve, in this way:

1. Estimate revenues for the fiscal year (or biennium) based on past trends, and then double or triple the estimates.
2. Set budget appropriations at the highest organizational level legally possible (e.g., total appropriation for a department), balanced to the (inflated) revenue estimates. This whole process could be done in at most a couple of hours, using a simple spreadsheet.
3. Stick the budget in a file somewhere, and forget about it. If the revenue estimates (and corresponding appropriations) are set high enough, actual spending is guaranteed to come in under budget. This is all that matters.

Note that this approach is appropriate *only if* it is used as an exercise to meet arbitrary and outdated requirements of state law, where the real financial management is done in a different (better way). Of course, "balancing" a budget based on intentionally-inflated revenue estimates is nothing new, even where the government does *not* follow a better, alternative process. This was how Ronald Reagan fulfilled a campaign promise to reduce the deficit without really doing anything about it.[72] Churches often do it too, but at least they have a more legitimate expectation for divine intervention in making the actual numbers somehow add up.

---

[72] David Stockman, *The Triumph Of Politics: The Inside Story of the Reagan Revolution*, Avon Books, 1987.

Conclusion

"It's clearly a budget. It's got a lot of numbers in it."
—George W. Bush

A discussion of public budgeting is usually confined to one of two contexts: a political process that attempts to tie policy decisions to the allocation of financial resources; or an accounting process in which appropriation amounts are simply data points in a system with a lot of numbers in it. It is rare to consider the internal budget rules and processes as an expression of a management philosophy. The "beyond budgeting," movement, as with the Theory Y approach described in this book, explicitly recognizes the importance of designing a process for managing financial resources that complements, rather than undermines, the things we have learned over the past half century about motivation and human relations. Consider the introductory statement of the "Beyond Budgeting Round Table":

When the Beyond Budgeting Round Table (BBRT) was established over ten years ago its vision was to find steering mechanisms that could replace budgeting and help to make organizations more adaptive to change. But its members quickly realized that management processes (the way we set goals, strategy, plans and budgets, allocate resources, coordinate actions, and measure, reward and control performance) with budgeting at their core were not neutral in terms of management thinking and behavior. In fact, these processes were designed to enable leaders to command

and control the actions of front-line people. Head office did not want managers to think or act on their own. In fact, they didn't want any surprises. So if leaders now wanted managers to be more responsive, innovative and ethical, what did they need to change? The answer was not about fixing a few problems. It required a new way of thinking about management. It meant designing a new coherent management model.

...The management model (how you set targets, recognize and reward people, plan actions, allocate resources and measure and control performance) is the primary driver of management thinking and behavior in organizations today and has a major influence on the bottom line. It is also the key to survival in turbulent times. And while recent times have been the most turbulent in living memory most companies continue to manage with performance management models that are annual, negotiated and fixed and that add too little value.[73]

This statement refers to "companies," but the comments could apply to governments just as well. At the beginning of the 21st century, both the private and public sectors need to find better ways to budget, or not to budget at all.

---

[73]Beyond Budgeting Round Table web site, http://www.bbrt.org/beyond-budgeting/beybud.html, accessed on 10/26/12.

APPENDIX A

THE USELESSNESS OF BUDGET TRICKS IN A THEORY Y ORGANIZATION

The games people play in traditional budget systems are discussed in Chapter 4. Many budget tricks are invoked during a budget request process, where departments compete with each other for a slice of the fixed budget pie. These tricks are eliminated with the use of budget targets in a Theory Y system.

In a theory X organization, operating managers must be given just enough money to run their department, and no more, because they will simply waste any additional resources. So another series of tricks is employed to convince the budget analysts that the department really *needs* the money. In a Theory Y organization, managers are expected to carry out governing board priorities as efficiently and effectively as possible. In this case, a decision that increase efficiency, and thus provides more resources for more or better service, is a good thing, not a nefarious plot to waste more taxpayer money.

The following summary shows how most of the 21

budget tricks of a traditional process are made obsolete in a Theory Y budget system.

1. Magic disappearing revenue. The budget just won't balance, but you don't want to cut spending. Just increase the revenue estimate to make it balance...and worry about it later.

Theory X response: Account for all revenues centrally, and have central finance staff perform all revenue estimates and projections.

Theory Y solution: Operating units (and internal units that bill other departments for service) are responsible, to the maximum extent possible, for both estimating revenues and dealing with revenue shortfalls. There is no benefit to over-estimating revenue. General revenues such as taxes will still need to be estimated centrally, but operating departments that depend on them will put pressure on the forecasters to estimate as accurately as possible.

2. The sacrificial lamb. The budget office asks for a list of programs that could be cut if spending reductions are necessary. The department head offers up the pet programs of the CEO or governing body (e.g., army base closures), knowing they will be held sacred. This is the oldest trick in the book, yet people keep doing it. (This trick is also known as the Washington Monument Syndrome: if the National Park Service is told to reduce its budget, the first thing it will propose to cut is operation of the popular Washington Monument).

Theory X response: When the tactic is too blatant, discipline the offending manager.

Theory Y solution: Governing board priorities are made clear well in advance of the budget process. Operating managers are given a total budget target to meet the board's priorities.

3. Groundhog Day. The police chief requests an additional traffic enforcement officer, promising that additional traffic tickets will pay for the position. Over the next few years, the position is shifted to other areas, and traffic enforcement drops off. The chief then requests an additional patrol officer, promising that additional traffic tickets will pay for the position.

Theory X response: Keep careful records during budget hearings in order to expose this trick and deny the request.

Theory Y solution: Not an issue in a Theory Y budget. There is no "budget request" process.

4. It's only routine replacement. The parks department scrounges some old surplus conference chairs and a table from another department. In the next budget cycle they include a request to replace the aging office equipment.

Theory X response: Create new rules allowing for replacement costs only when equipment was originally purchased through an approved budget line item.

Theory Y solution:Not an issue in a Theory Y budget. There is no "budget request" process.

5. Grants? What grants? The department adds a plug in the budget in case a grant is received. The grant application is unsuccessful, but the spending authority remains in the budget (and the money gets spent).

Theory X response: Centralize both revenues *and* expenditure budgets for grant-funded programs, to ensure that departments do not have access to the funds until the grant is secured.

Theory Y solution: All departments or programs, even those within the general fund, are self-balancing (budgeted expenditures equal estimated revenues). Bottom-line control means that total expenditures must always stay within total (actual) revenues. What this means in practice is that grant-based spending authority is created only when the grant is actually awarded.

6. Spend it or lose it. Another old trick, with many variants. The department has a goal of spending every penny in the budget, both to avoid losing it at the end of the fiscal year, and to prove to the pesky budget analysts that they really need every cent in their budget.

Theory X response: Institute an arbitrary (and unpredictable) cutoff date for requisitions, to catch departments off guard. Or provide extra scrutiny of requisitions near the end of the fiscal year, demanding thorough justification for each dollar spent.

Theory Y solution: The ability of departments to carry over 100% of their year-end savings ends this trick once and for all.

7. Don't ask, it's technical. The public works director slips in a request for a new riding lawn mower (for park maintenance), sandwiched between a twenty million dollar water plant upgrade and a ten million dollar sewer plant expansion. The city council members spend most of the budget hearing talking about their personal experience with lawn mowers, and gloss over the treatment plant budgets.

<u>Theory X response</u>: Allow the governing body to see only the total cost of the program; let the professionals (central staff) deal with the details since they are too sophisticated to be tricked like this.

<u>Theory Y solution</u>: Because there is no budget request process, games like this are pointless. Managers are paid to manage, and this includes managing their budgets.

8. The myth of the "current services" budget. The department increases next year's budget by a combination of inflation and population growth, conveniently ignoring economies of scale, substitution of different goods and services, and the fact that not all costs follow the Consumer Price Index.

<u>Theory X response</u>: Entrust central department staff with the task of constructing complex forecasting models to ascertain the "true" cost increase.

<u>Theory Y solution</u>: The line item budgets developed by the operating departments (that add up to the total budget target) are for planning purposes only. They will be held accountable for the bottom line *actual* results. They may use a variety of techniques to estimate future revenues and costs (and they may be receptive to help from central financial experts in doing this). The CEO or budget director typically uses some kind of formula as a starting point to establish the departments' spending targets and will need to use judgment in how to address inflationary pressure.

9. The moving target. Major capital improvement projects (e.g., roads, buildings) are done over several years. Few budget systems track total spending versus the original budget over multiple years, making it easy for the manager to hide the true cost of the project.

Theory X response: Establish central multi-year tracking systems for capital improvements, and give project managers an annual allotment, making sure the allotment for the final year guarantees the project will remain within the original budget.

Theory Y solution: The Theory Y process described here focuses on the operating, not capital budgets, and thus does not address this problem. It is simply one more weakness of the traditional annual budget (appropriations) process. Capital improvements should be budgeted on a project basis, spanning as many years as necessary to complete the project, and as with Theory Y operating budgets, control should be on the bottom line (project expenditures must be covered by revenue), not simply on the relationship between actual and *estimated* costs.

10. Spending the savings. New equipment is requested in the budget on the basis of future operating savings. Somehow the manager forgets to request a smaller budget in future years.

Theory X response: Keep careful notes during the budget process, and cut the department's budget in the future when the promised savings are supposed to occur.

Theory Y solution: Managers have a built-in incentive to make investments that will reduce future costs, since they don't need to worry that the savings will be "taken" from them and shifted to some other department. This allows them to increase or preserve service levels within the manager's area of responsibility, and the citizen or customer benefits.

11. Going to the well. A senior employee retires, yielding an unexpected windfall in salary savings that the department manager shifts somewhere else. But when the air conditioning system goes out, she asks the Board of Commissioners for a transfer from the general fund contingency account.

Theory X response: Assign the central budget analyst the task of poring over the department's budget to see if the air conditioner can be purchased out of savings, and to verify the accuracy of the department's estimate of the cost of the air conditioner.

Theory Y response: Departments carry their own contingency accounts, and within reason, must deal with unexpected budget challenges themselves. In unusual circumstances, the manager may need help (additional funds) to deal with a large shock to the budget; in this case, he or she will need to prove that the need is justified.

12. If it saves just one life. This simple phrase has been used to justify all sorts of dubious spending on equipment and personnel by fire departments and other public safety agencies.

Theory X response: When the fire chief says, "you can't put a price on a life," bring in an actuary to point out that, yes, you can.

Theory Y solution: Once the total fire budget target is set, the chief is responsible for setting priorities within the department and will be more resistant to unfounded justifications for equipment or programs. The governing boards of local governments may well set a higher priority for fire and police services (in comparison to services that benefit more citizens) than is necessary, but that is their prerogative.

13. The old switcheroo. The department manager argues hard (and successfully) for the expensive piece of equipment they must have to do the job properly. When the ink is dry on the final budget, the manager buys the cheaper item that he knew all along would work, and spends the savings somewhere else.

Theory X response: Budget for the (expensive) equipment in a separate line item, and prohibit any savings from being spent elsewhere.

Theory Y solution: Another game that is eliminated by the lack of a budget request process.

14. Look what we found. In a variation of #13, the department gets budget approval to replace the motor pool car. They discover that they can, in fact, keep the old car running another year, and spend the appropriation elsewhere. Next year they request funds to replace the pool car.

Theory X response: Keep careful notes during the budget process, and discipline the department manager when this trick is used (the employee's annual performance review, nine months later, would be a good time to do this).

Theory Y solution: See #13 above.

15. Poor me. The department makes a show of its run-down equipment and office furniture, to prove to policy makers how under-funded it is.

Theory X response: Criticize the department for not taking better care of its equipment.

Theory Y solution: This tactic might still work: the CEO or budget director will consider the overall financial condition of the department in setting budget targets. But due to the bottom-line focus, the department will need to be stretched thin in all areas to receive any sympathy. The tactic won't work if the run down office furniture is occupied by more staff than is needed.

16. The nose under the tent. The manager budgets for a new position, starting in the last quarter of the fiscal year. The salary and fringe cost seems modest enough, but the full impact is hidden until the next fiscal year, at which time the program is up and running with a new group of clients.

Theory X response: This is just the cost of doing business.

Theory Y solution: It is the operating manager, not the central budget staff, who will have to deal with the future consequences of this kind of action. If he or she is confident that the cost can be absorbed, then the manager should be free to make staffing changes whenever necessary.

17. The gift that keeps on giving. The police chief argues successfully for a new officer. The budget includes recurring salary and operating costs, and one-time costs for a car and radios. The one-time costs are magically rolled into the regular budget request the next year.

Theory X response: Keep careful notes during the budget process, and reduce next year's budget by the cost of the car and radios.

Theory Y solution: Another trick eliminated by using bottom-line budget targets rather than a budget request carnival.

18. The accountants made me do it. Line items with obscure or unusual names (merchant fees, ODEQ regulatory fees) are padded, knowing that the simple ones (travel, office supplies) are the only ones that will be attacked.

Theory X response: Hire central budget analysts to examine the use of these line items, and challenge department's budget estimates.

Theory Y solution: Line item estimates are used for planning purposes only (internal to the department). There is no incentive to pad or otherwise play games with these estimates.

19. Whoops, where did it go? A new program is proposed that will be supported by user fees. Near the end of the process, the manager "sacrifices" the program for a smaller expenditure (except that the smaller program generates no user fees).

Theory X response: Again, hire central budget analysts to keep on top of issues like this.

Theory Y solution: Controlling to the bottom line (expenditures less than or equal to revenues) eliminates this trick.

20. The long sunset. A five-year lease purchase payment ends. Strangely, the amount stays in the budget for several more years.

Theory X response: Maintain a large and detailed central tickler file to remind central budget managers when departmental budget items are no longer justified.

Theory Y solution: This gives the operating manager more flexibility or resources to provide services to citizens. How can this be a bad thing?

21. If it's the private sector, it must be efficient. High salaries and expensive equipment are hidden in a lump sum private contract payment; no one can see the line items.

Theory X response: Insist on cost-plus contracts, where the agency must review and approve the line item expenses of the contractor.

Theory Y solution: See #18, above. Since these contract costs come out of the department's bottom line, the operating manager will have a strong incentive to make sure they're getting good value for the money.

SCOTT DOUGLAS LAZENBY

ABOUT THE AUTHOR

Scott Lazenby has been a city manager in Oregon for over two decades, and previously served as management and budget director for a large Arizona city. He also teaches public administration as an adjunct professor for Portland State University. He has a BA in physics from Reed College, an MS in public management & policy from Carnegie-Mellon University, and a PhD in public administration & policy from the Hatfield School of Government at Portland State. He is the author of several fiction books, including the city management novel, *Playing With Fire* and the soon-to-be-released *State of the City*.

Contact him via www.scottlazenbybooks.com

ABOUT EREHWON PRESS

Debt-ridden college students have a hard time paying the high prices charged for books by traditional textbook publishers. To keep this one affordable, Erehwon Press (the author's own publishing business) handled the typesetting and cover design. Printing, sales, and distribution are done by Amazon's CreateSpace company. The book is available for all major ebook platforms, also at very reasonable prices.

For more information, see erehwonpress.com

13423809R00100

Made in the USA
San Bernardino, CA
13 December 2018